ROYAL MUSEUMS GREENWICH

The Queen's House

Souvenir Guide

First published in 2021 by the National Maritime Museum, Park Row, Greenwich, London SE10 9NF. This edition published in 2022.

978-1-906367-72-5

Original text by Pieter van der Merwe: updated and expanded for this edition by Allison Goudie
Designed by louiseturpindesign.co.uk

A CIP catalogue record for this book is available from the British Library.

Printed and bound in the UK by L&S Printing
10 9 8 7 6 5 4 3 2

This guidebook is updated periodically but please note that visitor information is liable to change. Due to rotations and objects on loan, some artworks featured in this book may not be in the expected location or may have been removed from the Queen's House.

MIX
Paper | Supporting responsible forestry
FSC
www.fsc.org
FSC® C014531

Contents

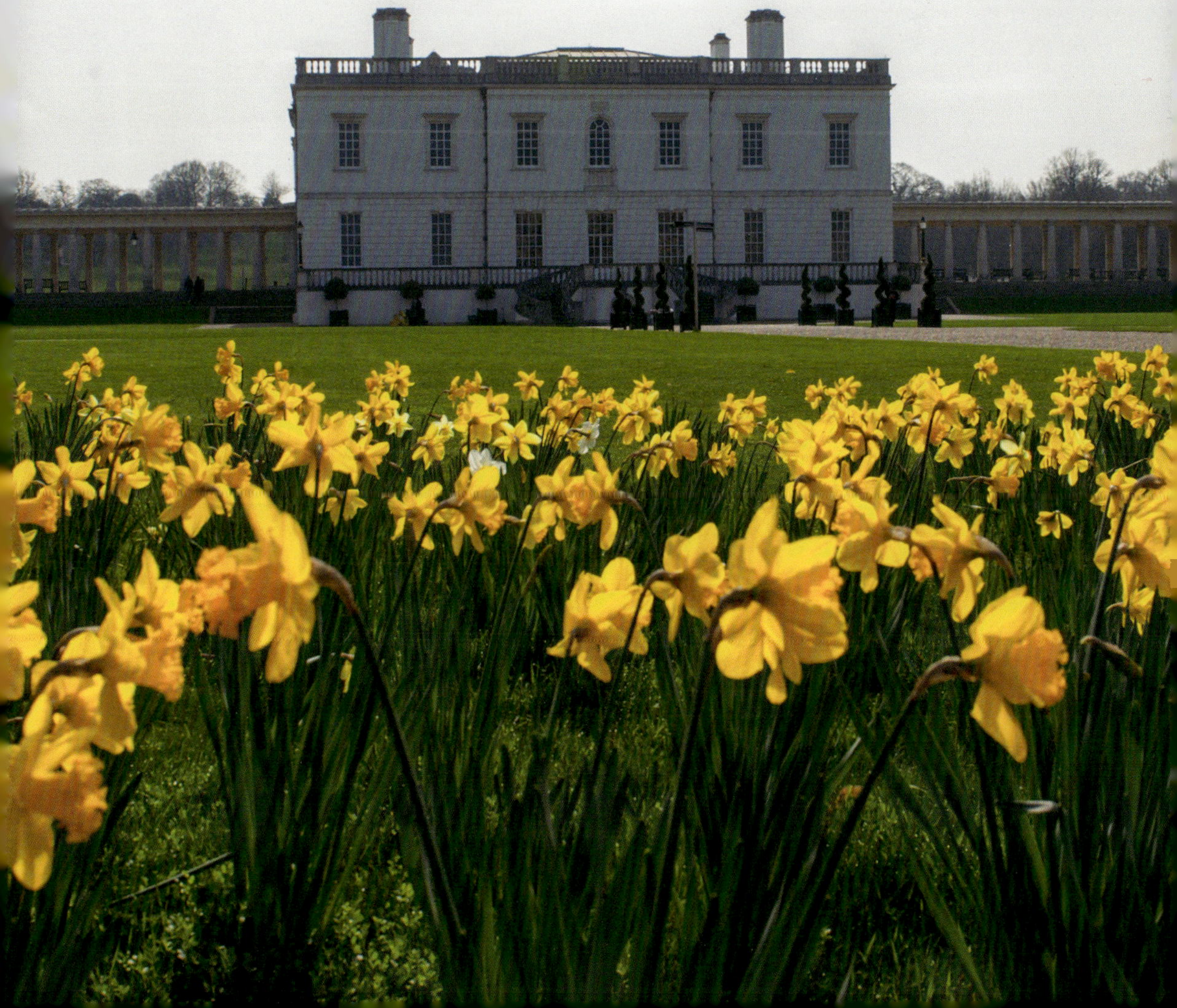

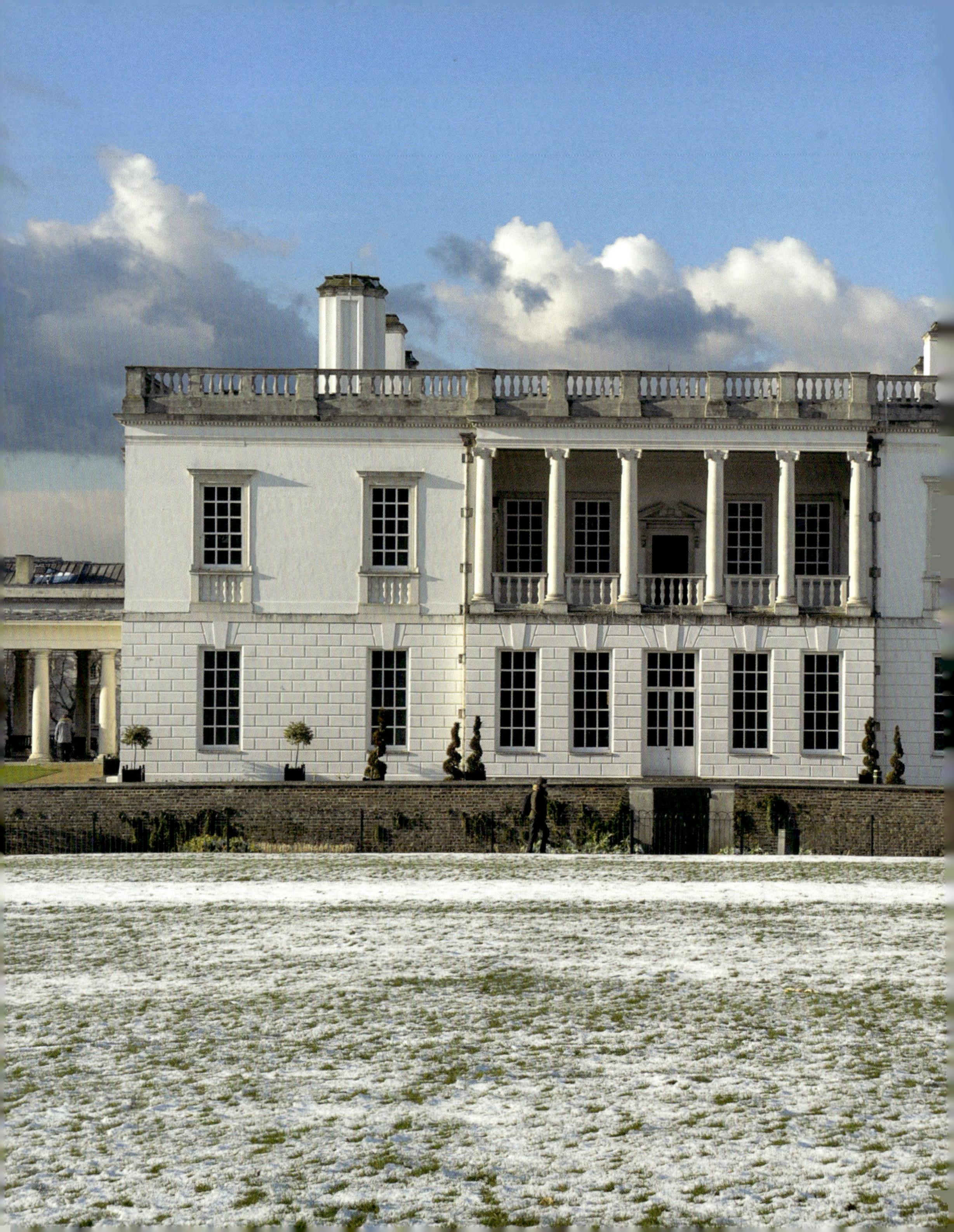

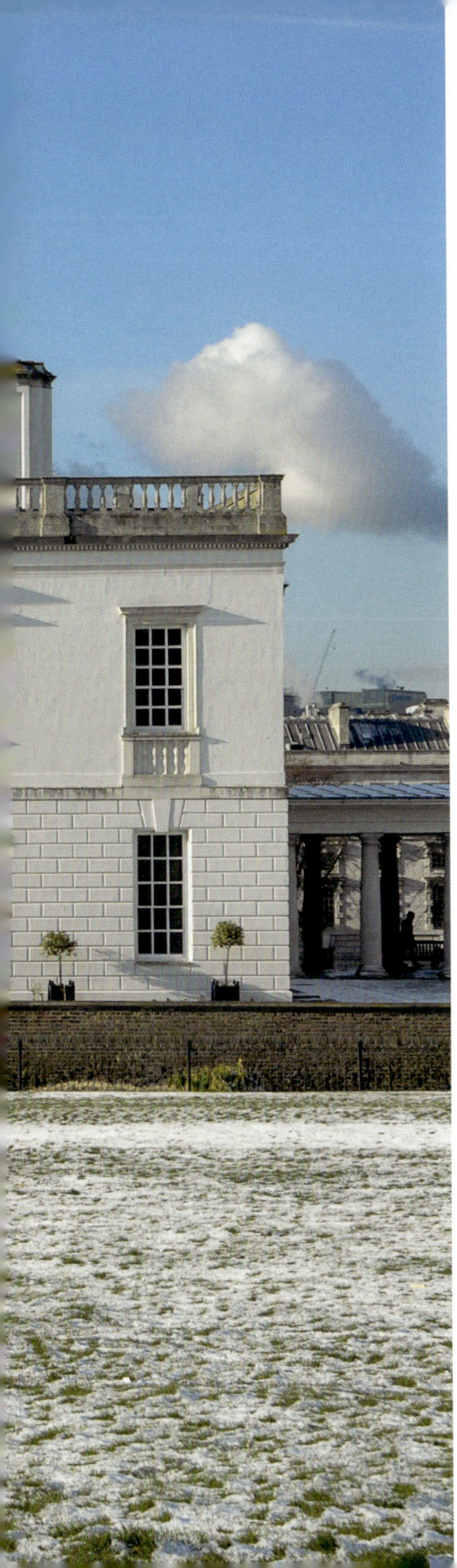

Introduction

The Queen's House is an extraordinary place. One of the most important buildings in the country, this 'house of delight' was at the cutting edge of art and architecture when it was completed for Queen Henrietta Maria in the 1630s. It is the last architectural addition to, and now last remnant of, the sprawling Tudor palace of Greenwich, and the point of origin for the later architectural development of Greenwich in the 17th and 18th centuries. Its remarkable history since then has seen it play host to artists' studio, school accommodation and Women's Royal Naval Service wartime quarters.

In early 2012, marking Her Majesty Queen Elizabeth II's Diamond Jubilee year, the London Borough of Greenwich was granted royal status, becoming the Royal Borough of Greenwich. The Royal Household emphasised at the time that the honour was 'a very rare and exceptional mark of Royal favour'. This privilege reflected Greenwich's long and close association with the monarchy, stretching back to the late 15th century. The Queen's House is very much the touchstone for Greenwich's royal story.

Today, the House is home to a magnificent art collection, from old-master paintings to contemporary installations, accompanied by a vibrant public programme of concerts and talks – a house of delight for the 21st century.

◀ *South exterior of the Queen's House from Greenwich Park.*

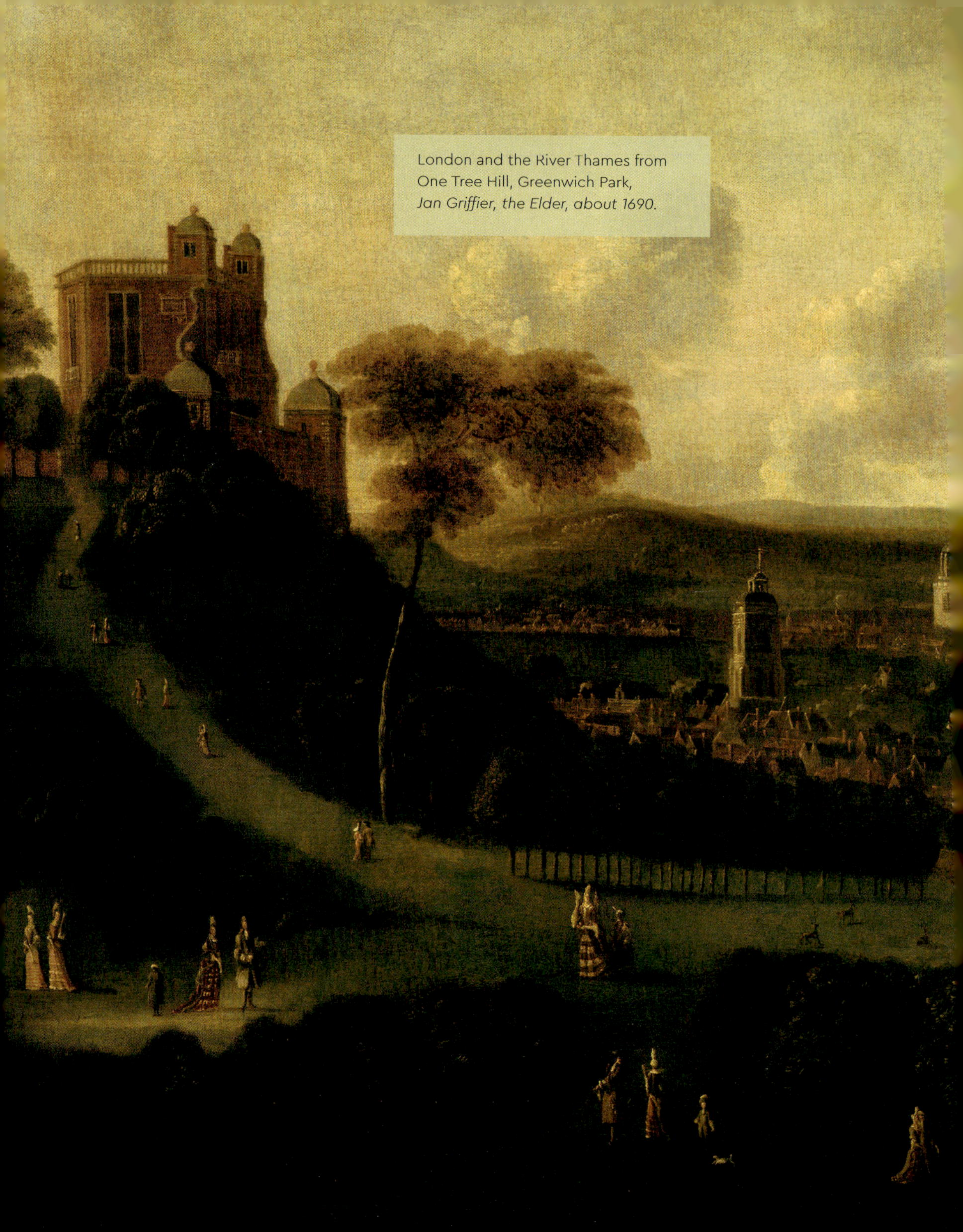

London and the River Thames from One Tree Hill, Greenwich Park, *Jan Griffier, the Elder, about 1690.*

History of the Queen's House

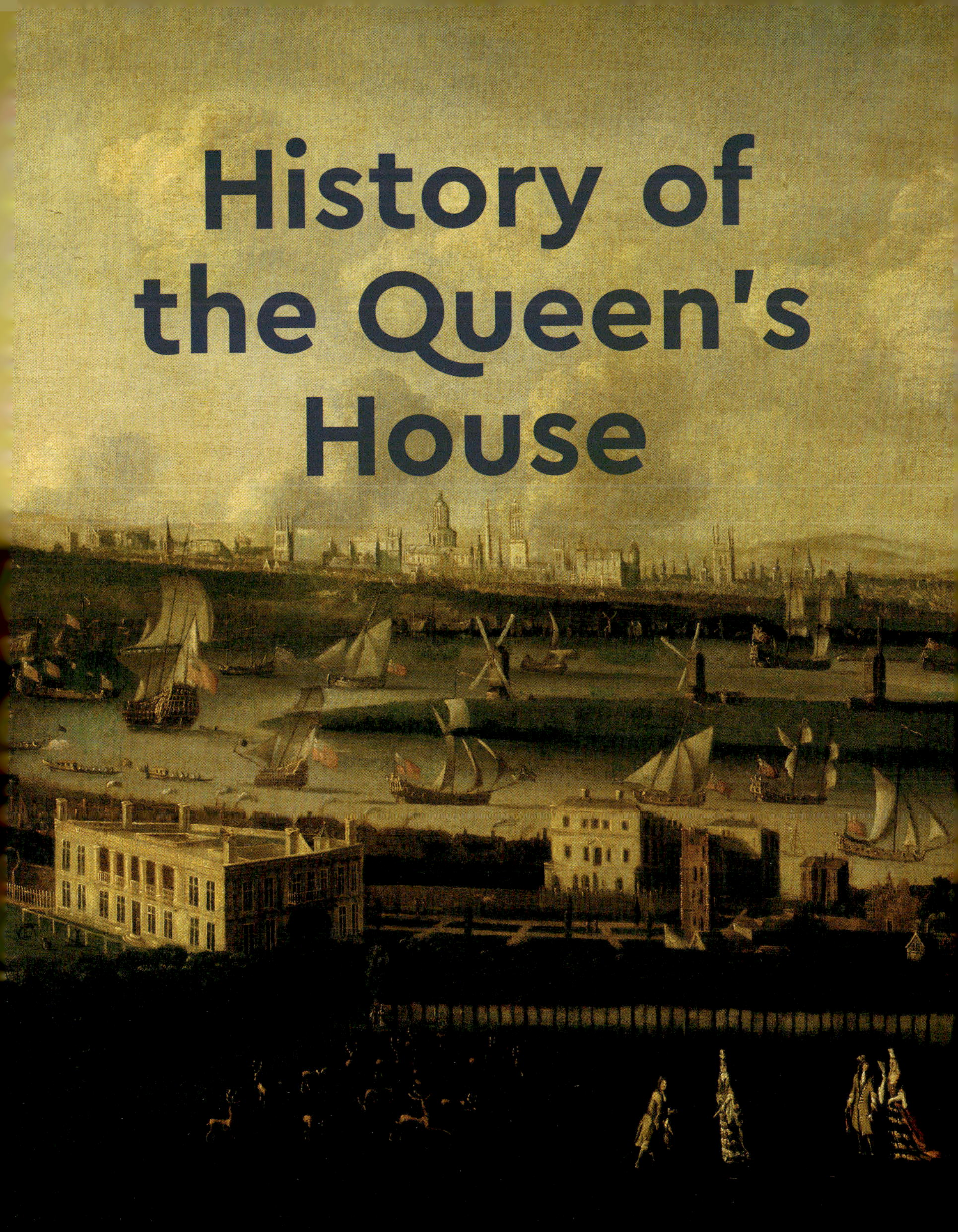

The Queen's House through time

1426–33: Manor of Bellacourt built by Humphrey, Duke of Gloucester

1447–52: Margaret of Anjou redevelops Bellacourt as her 'Pleasaunce' or Palace of Placentia

1400s

1491: Henry VIII born at Placentia

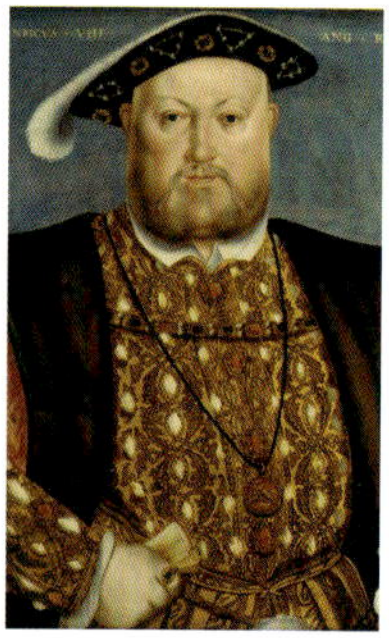

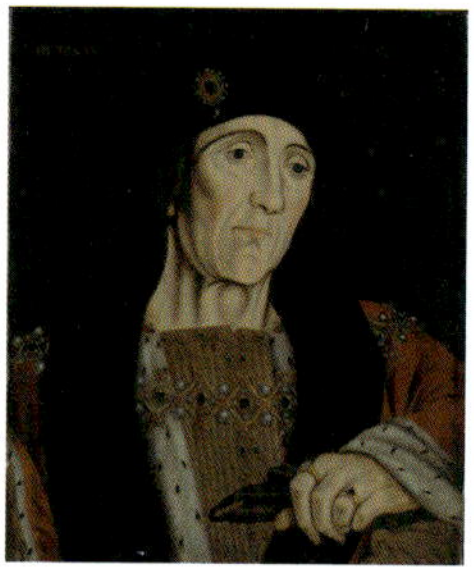

1498–1504: Greenwich Palace constructed under Henry VII and Elizabeth of York, replacing Placentia

1516: Mary I born at Greenwich Palace

1533: Elizabeth I born at Greenwich Palace

1500s

1587: Elizabeth I signs execution warrant for Mary, Queen of Scots, at Greenwich

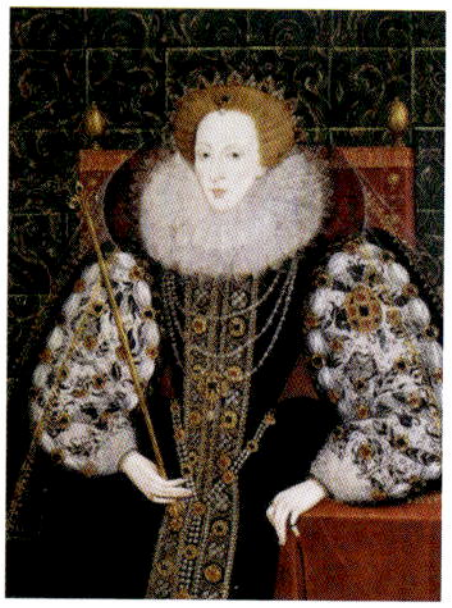

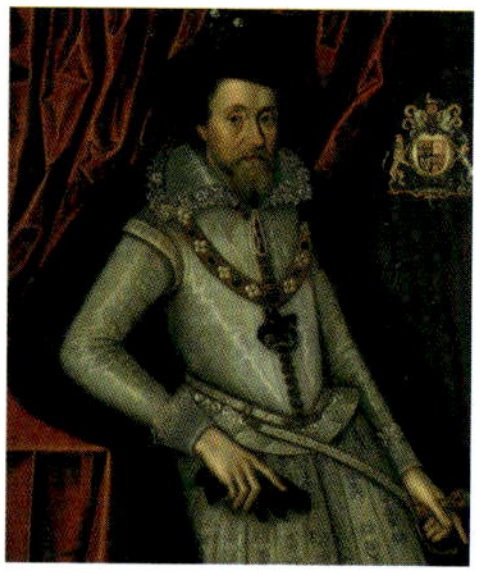

1613: James I gives manor of Greenwich to his wife, Anne of Denmark

1616: Anne of Denmark commissions the Queen's House from Inigo Jones: work begins in 1617

1618: Work stops with House half-built: Anne dies in 1619

1632: Work recommences on the Queen's House under Queen Henrietta Maria, wife of Charles I

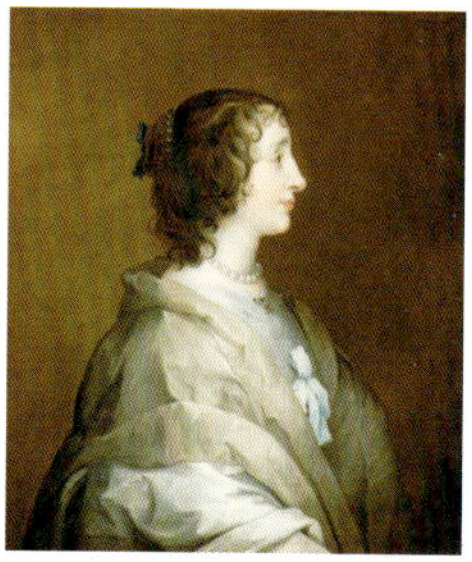

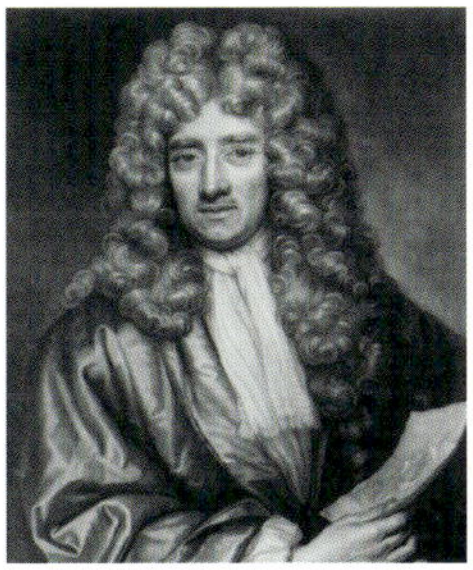

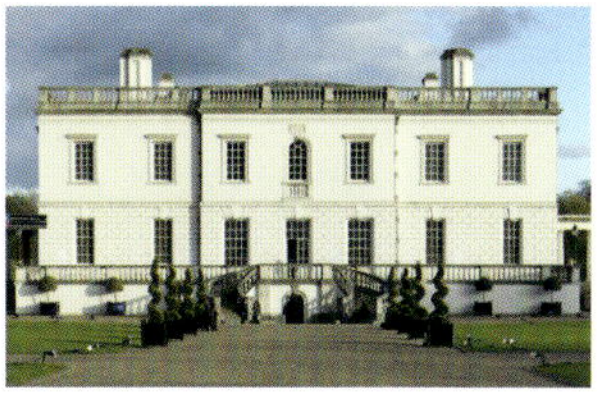

1635: Queen's House structurally complete; interior finished about 1638. Henrietta Maria in exile in France from 1644 following the outbreak of the Civil War in 1642

1673–74: Willem van de Velde the Elder and Younger given a studio in the Queen's House by Charles II

1807–09: The Royal Naval Asylum moves into the Queen's House and new adjoining wings. Combines with Greenwich Hospital School from 1821, is renamed Royal Hospital School in 1892 and moves to Suffolk in 1933

1986–90: Second major restoration, services refit and re-presentation. 'Horseshoe stairs' entrance approach remodelled and lift inserted in 1999 to improve disability access

1600s 1700s 1800s 1900s 2000s

1649: Charles I executed. Queen's House, Palace of Greenwich and their contents seized by the Commonwealth

1661–62: Charles II (restored to the throne in 1660) adds the East and West Bridge Rooms of the Queen's House

1743–80: Queen's House occupied by Lady Katharine Pelham, its longest resident

1937: After major restoration, the Queen's House opens to the public as part of the National Maritime Museum

2016: Queen's House celebrates the 400th anniversary of its design with a third refurbishment and re-presentation project

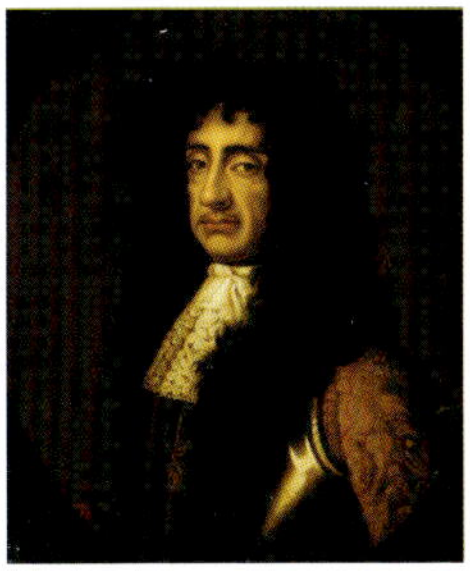

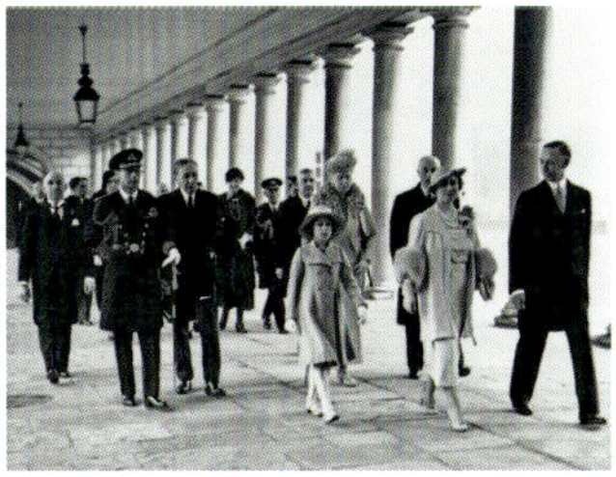

Greenwich Palace

Modern visitors to Greenwich are often struck by the contrast between the glass and steel skyscrapers of Canary Wharf across the River Thames and the overwhelmingly neo-classical architectural landscape of the 17th- and 18th-century Maritime Greenwich UNESCO World Heritage Site. Once, however, it was the buildings now comprising the World Heritage Site which represented the latest in cutting-edge architectural design, presenting an equally stark contrast with their surroundings. At its completion in 1635 the bright white edifice of the Queen's House, the first Palladian building in England, would have gleamed against the much older red-brick Tudor palace complex into which it had been inserted.

Around 1600, in the final years of the reign of Elizabeth I, an observer standing on the opposite bank of the Thames would have seen the low unbroken panorama of the red-brick Palace of Greenwich filling the area where the Old Royal Naval College now stands, hugging the foreshore with a narrow river walk under its long north frontage. This vista was punctuated

▼ Greenwich Palace from the north-east with a man-of-war, *Netherlandish School, about 1630. The twin towers of Henry VIII's tiltyard can be seen in the centre, with the square tower that held the king's private apartments on the far right.*

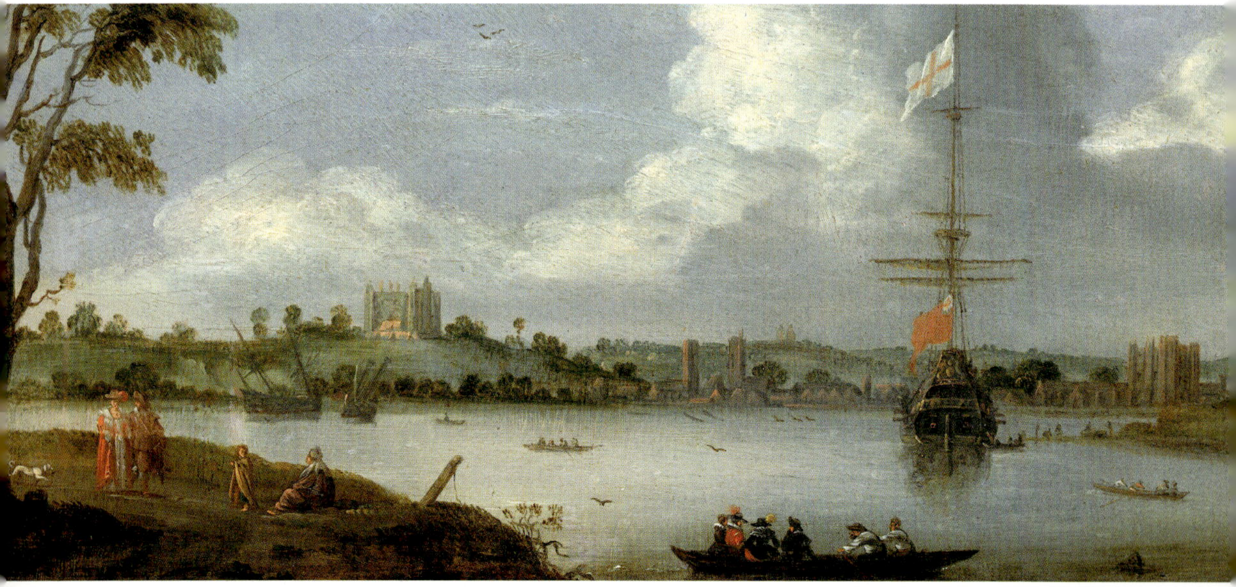

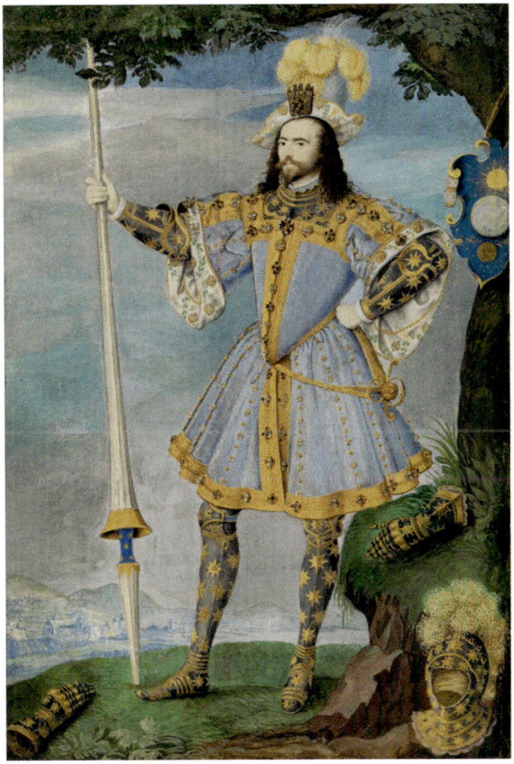

George Clifford, 3rd Earl of Cumberland, (1558–1605), *Nicholas Hilliard, about 1590. Thought to have been created to mark Clifford's promotion to the role of Elizabeth I's champion, this miniature shows Clifford with elaborate tournament armour made at the Greenwich armoury established by Henry VIII.*

by two dominant structures: a square tower, holding the king's private apartments, and, further east, the Chapel, beyond which extended King Henry VIII's tiltyard, where jousting tournaments were held. Behind this, separated from the palace complex by the walled road connecting Woolwich and Deptford running along what are now the east–west colonnades on either side of the Queen's House, was the Royal Park, well-stocked with deer for royal hunting.

The Tudor palace was originally established under Henry VII, who rebuilt and redeveloped it, to a design envisaged by his queen Elizabeth of York, on the site of an earlier medieval palace and monastic buildings. Under Henry VIII, Greenwich Palace was expanded and enhanced, serving as his principal London residence and the seat of royal power and ceremony for the first two decades of his reign. Henry VIII created an elaborate infrastructure for royal ceremonial and entertainment: the tiltyard was bordered by banqueting and 'disguising' houses, the latter for elaborate court spectacles called masques. The complex was further serviced by impressive stables and a famous armoury. The armoury in particular illustrates one of the many ways in which Henry VIII attempted both to emulate European rivals and to impress his status on them. Prior to the

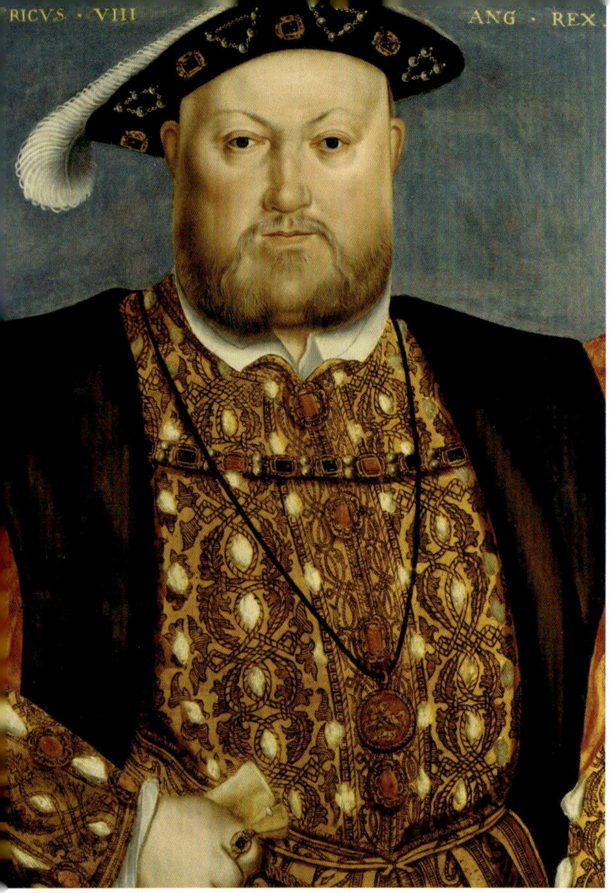

▲ Henry VIII (1491–1547), *studio of Hans Holbein, 16th century.*

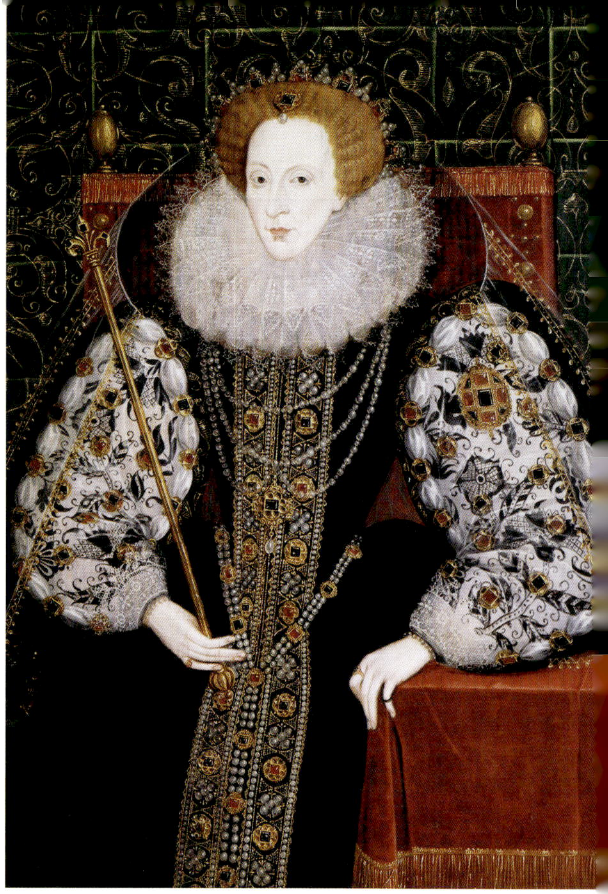

▲ Elizabeth I (1533–1603), *British school, 16th century.*

establishment of the royal armoury at Greenwich Palace, fine ceremonial armour had to be imported from Continental Europe. By establishing the armoury at Greenwich, Henry opted instead to 'import' the talent responsible for it, persuading expert armourers from Germany, Italy and the Low Countries to come to England in his service and produce armour of the highest quality.

Greenwich was intimately connected with the Tudor dynasty. It was at Greenwich that Henry VIII was born, but in the old palace; so were his daughters Mary I and Elizabeth I, in the redeveloped Tudor one. It was also here that Elizabeth's mother, Anne Boleyn, was arrested for treason on Henry's orders in 1536 before being taken up-river to the Tower of London, where she was imprisoned, tried and executed. Henry's immediate successor, his son Edward VI, who died at Greenwich in 1553, made great use of the palace as did both Mary I and Elizabeth I, especially in summer. It was at Greenwich that Elizabeth watched the return of the *Golden Hind* after Sir Francis Drake's circumnavigation of the globe in 1577–80, and received royal salutes from passing ships – until the practice was stopped after a shot from an accidentally loaded gun smashed one of her private windows. In February 1587, it was 'from Greenwich, in haste' that Elizabeth's Council finally sent out her signed execution warrant for Mary, Queen of Scots.

As monarch in her own right, and unmarried, Elizabeth mainly occupied her father's apartments along the river, rather than those of his successive queens to the south. She was known to use a gatehouse on the southern perimeter of the palace complex, which connected the palace to the adjacent royal park by straddling the walled Woolwich to Deptford road, to watch events in the park. The gatehouse appears to have been close to, if not partly overlapping the west side of the Queen's House, and was demolished for the House to be built. Despite having an upper chamber with a large window on the park, it is not clear if it acted as a covered bridge over the road. It was certainly not a formal 'royal' one and it has been suggested that the gated crossing below has a claim to be where Sir Walter Raleigh famously ruined his cloak to allow Elizabeth to pass dry-shod when he first came to court in 1582.

In an age in which most international visitors travelled to London by ship, Greenwich Palace was the first major royal site they encountered and therefore ideally placed for official welcomes, and equally ceremonious departures. Even when important visitors arrived by land from Dover the same applied, since the Dover road passed close to Greenwich. Indeed, the royal site of Greenwich continued to be used for such diplomatic purposes, notably when royal yachts were involved as transport, into the early 1800s and long after the Tudor palace disappeared.

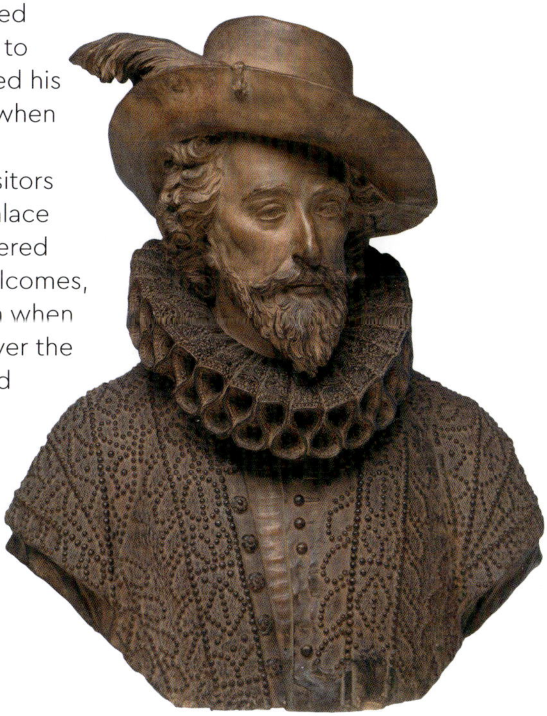

A terracotta bust of Sir Walter Raleigh (1552–1618), *John Michael Rysbrack, 1757.*

Inigo Jones and the early Stuart court

In 1613 James I, Elizabeth I's successor, gave the manor of Greenwich (which included the palace) to his Danish queen, Anne. Anne was a keen huntswoman, and it was reported that the king gave Greenwich to her (plus a costly diamond) in apology for losing his temper after she accidentally shot his favourite dog while hunting. He had already made early improvements to the queen's apartments on the south side of the palace, and had the celebrated engineer and garden designer Salomon de Caus update Elizabeth I's gardens in the Italian style, complete with fountains and a grotto.

In June 1617, the courtier John Chamberlain reported that 'The Queen ... is building somewhat at Greenwich, wch must be finished this sommer, yt is saide to be some curious devise of Inigo Jones, and will cost above 4000li ...' This is an appropriate first reference to the Queen's House, the design of which Jones began in October 1616, for 'curious' then meant 'elegant' or 'finished', and 'devise' (device) primarily had a heraldic meaning, suggesting

▼ Inigo Jones (1573–1652), *William Dobson, about 1642.*

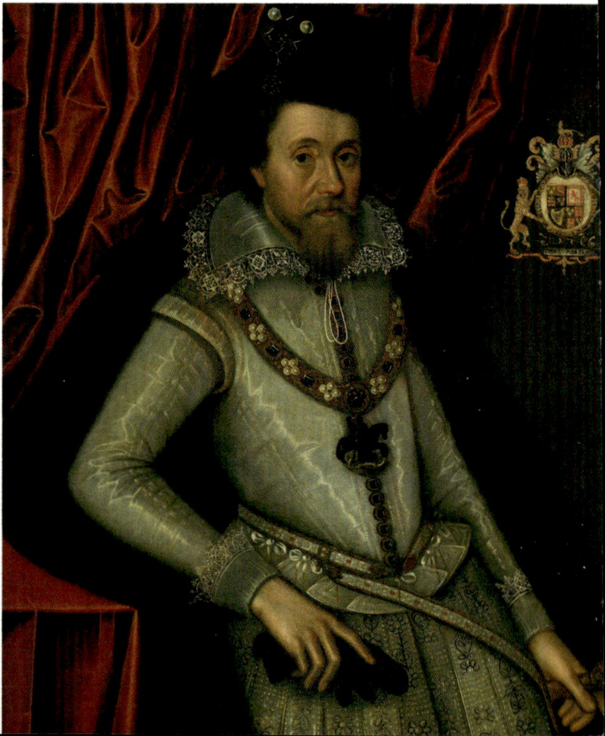

▼ James I (1566–1625), *John de Critz, about 1610.*

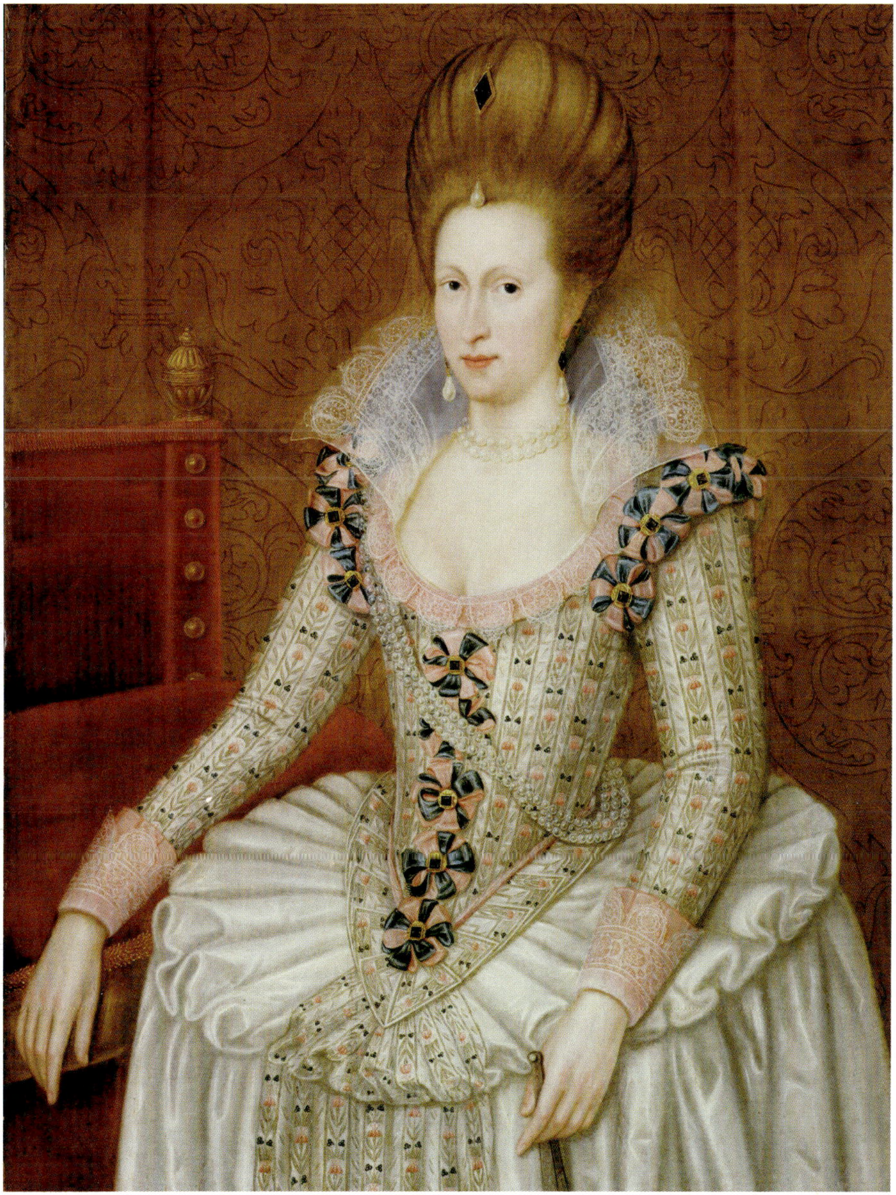

Anne of Denmark (1574–1619), *the studio of John de Critz, about 1605.*

an emblem which represented the qualities or aspirations of its owner. Both Chamberlain's description and Jones's involvement suggest that Anne's intention for the building was that it should be a site for the performance of her own ceremonial and the display of her own self-image. Jones had made his name as a designer and producer of court masques; elaborate allegorical and audience-participatory entertainments that glorified the Crown, in which Anne herself often participated. By the time the Queen's House was commissioned, Anne's court was not only distinct, but rather estranged from, and even at times in competition with the king's. Jones's design for Anne's projected Queen's House was, like the masques she so enjoyed, intended as an expression of the splendour and significance of her court in this atmosphere of competitive tension. Jones's Banqueting House in Whitehall (finished in 1622), built for the masques of James's court, was intended to reflect his competing majesty but neither building was completed until after Anne's death.

The design of the Queen's House improved the function of the old Tudor gatehouse, providing an elegant, private solution to the practical matter of crossing the public road that separated the Tudor palace from the park to the south. It also created a focal point for activities in the park such as hunting. Given the external design of the Queen's House, and some of its internal detail, it is now clear that Jones conceived the House's southern, sun-facing side as the 'front'. Anne was acutely aware both of her impressive dynastic pedigree, which connected her to royal families throughout Europe, and of her role as a patron and *amateur* (connoisseur and enthusiast) of the contemporary arts in their various forms. The Queen's House was perhaps therefore intended to impose a cosmopolitan, 'modern' frontispiece to the late-medieval red-brick palace, when seen from the park and especially the hill above. This symbolic portal, with its white, classically ordered perfection would also have asserted the Queen's primacy as manorial chatelaine or 'mistress' of Greenwich. This role probably included ceremonious passage between palace and park, with the House's south loggia designed to provide a prestigious vantage from which she and important guests could both see and be seen.

Sadly, neither Anne nor the House got that far: she died of tuberculosis in March 1619, aged 44, and it was perhaps on account of her declining health

▶ Henrietta Maria (1609–69), *studio of Sir Anthony van Dyck, about 1638.*

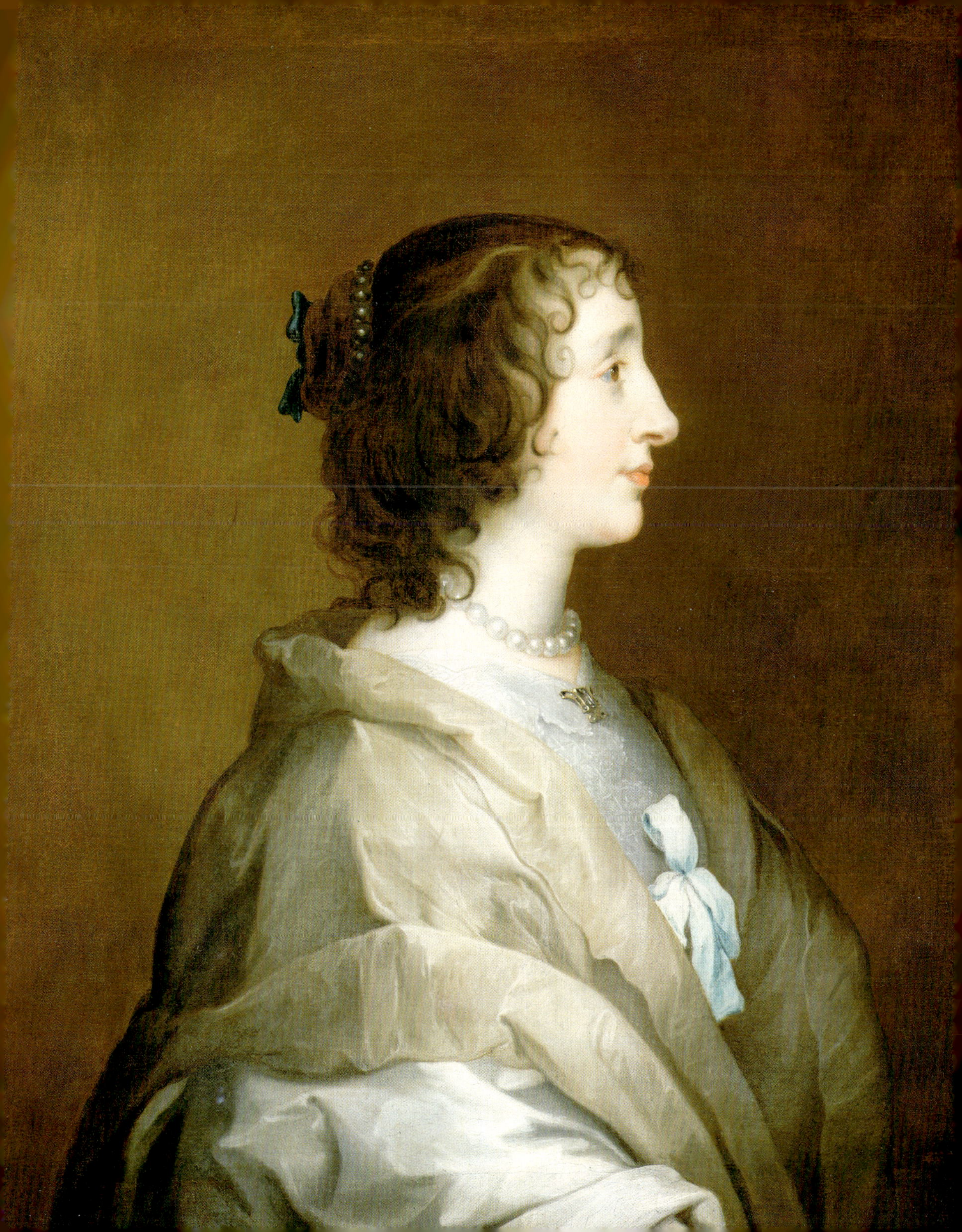

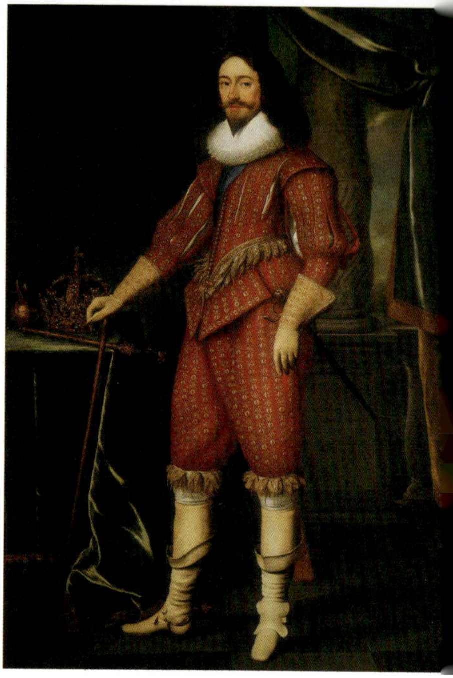

▲ Charles I (1600–49), *studio of Daniel Mytens the Elder, about 1631.*

that work had stopped in April 1618, when the House's two separate ground-floor storeys were left as brick shells. The half-built storeys remained, thatched over, until Charles I in turn vested Greenwich in his French wife, Henrietta Maria, in 1629. Like Anne, Henrietta Maria was a leader of fashion and the arts, whose connections with Catholic Europe gave her privileged access to the best European painters of the day. However, this also meant her patronage was at times enmeshed in religious politics, doing little for her popularity in Protestant England, which viewed her devout and rather overt Catholicism with disapproval.

Work on the House recommenced for Henrietta Maria in 1632, still under the direction of Inigo Jones, who had outlived both Anne of Denmark and James I. The structure was completed in 1635, with the two-storey ranges north and south of the road linked by a single central bridge. The major addition was the north terrace, to afford a better view over the palace gardens that had again been remodelled by the new queen. This marked the start of the north side's role as the dominant public front of the House, as it is today, and was in keeping with Henrietta Maria's probable use of it as a more private villa, looking inward on the palace, than Anne had originally intended. By the end of the 1630s the principal interiors were lavishly decorated with sculpture and specially commissioned paintings, although some paintings intended for the House were never delivered as the political situation in England deteriorated with the approach of civil war.

Henrietta Maria's enjoyment of her House was short-lived. She and Charles were last briefly at Greenwich Palace in September 1642, before she took their daughter Mary to Holland to marry the Prince of Orange and raise money for the royalist cause. In 1644, as the Civil War developed, Henrietta Maria finally escaped to France. Nevertheless, in 1659, even after ten years of Puritan republican rule under Oliver Cromwell, memory of the 'house of delight' still lingered as one 'which Queen Mary [Henrietta Maria] ... so finished and furnished, that it far surpasseth all other of that kind in England'.

The Commonwealth and Restoration

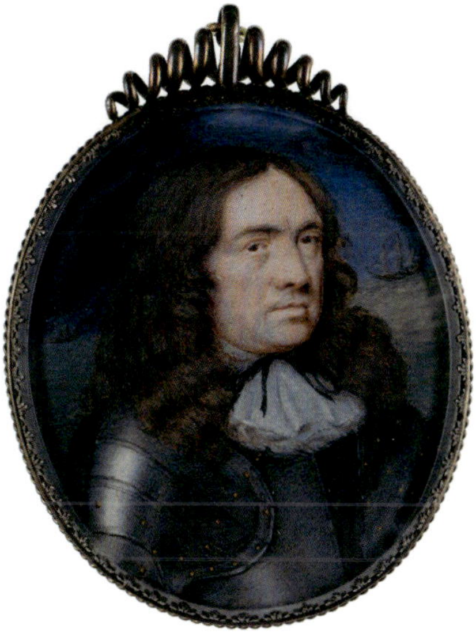

▲ Robert Blake, General at Sea (1599–1657), *Samuel Cooper, early 1650s.*

After Charles I's execution in 1649, Parliament sold 'the late King's goods', including the artworks from Greenwich. While the old Tudor Palace fell into decay during the Puritan Commonwealth, the Queen's House was reserved for Government use, though this did not render it immune from some degree of neglect and vandalism. A Dutch visitor to the Queen's House in 1674 commented on the condition of the fire surrounds: 'the marble leafwork mutilated: the noses of all the faces cut off from love of mischief, committed in the times of Cromwell'. Late in 1653, Oliver Cromwell briefly considered occupying the Queen's House himself, but this never came to fruition. Its only official use was for the lying-in-state in the Great Hall of two Parliamentary Generals at Sea: Richard Deane in 1653, killed in the First Anglo-Dutch War (which also saw prisoners detained in the old palace complex); and Robert Blake in 1657, after he died off Portsmouth on his return from victory against the Spanish.

The Restoration in 1660 brought renewed attention to the House. Charles II recognised the potential of Greenwich for grandiose redevelopment on the river highway into London. As his father and grandfather had done before him, he eventually vested the House in his queen, Catherine of Braganza, in 1670. However, initial improvements were made to the House to upgrade it for its first royal inhabitant, Henrietta Maria, Charles II's mother and now Queen Dowager. These works were probably well overdue. On his return to England, Charles II was told by Zachary Plott, a former Greenwich servant, that 'the Queen Mother's buildings ... are now employed to Entertain rude and debauched persons to drink and revel on Sabbath days'. Despite this, the Greenwich under-housekeeper, Uriah (or Vere) Babington, who had been in charge since 1634, managed to have his appointment renewed.

August 1661 saw work start on the addition of the House's East and West Bridge Rooms. Exactly who designed them is unclear, but 'draughts' were

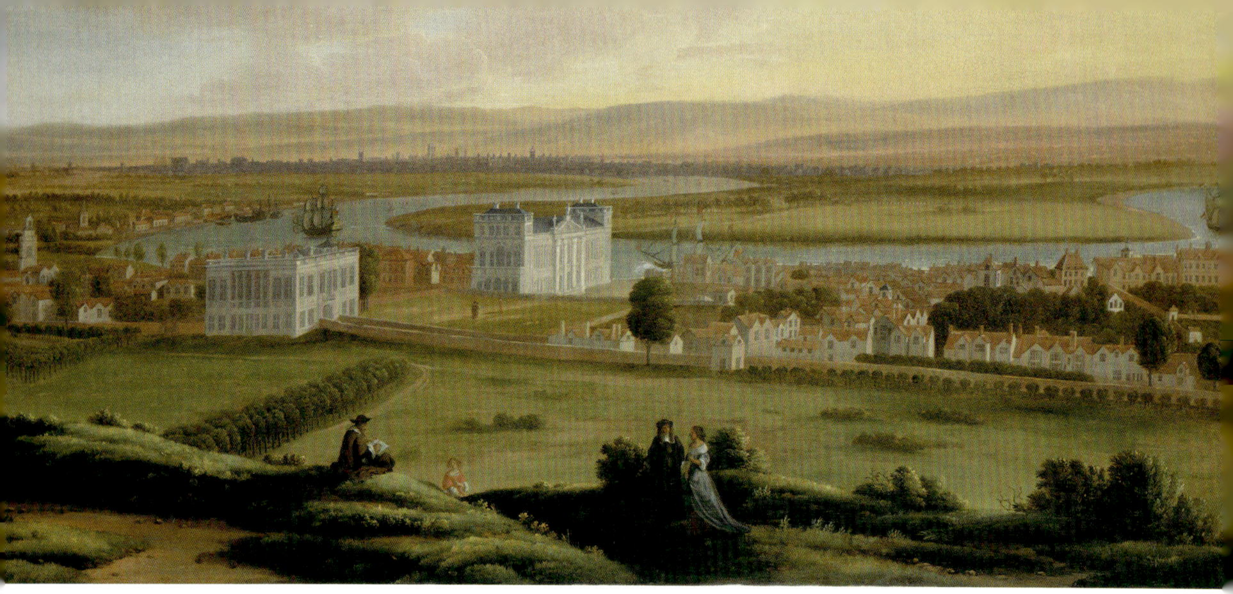

▲ A view of Greenwich and the Queen's House from the south east, *Hendrick Danckerts, about 1670. This painting shows the Queen's House with the recently added East (and West) Bridge Rooms, which gave the upper floor the fully connected square plan it has today.*

prepared by the Dutch architect Willem de Keyser. The bridges gave the upper floor today's fully connected square plan, with 'King's Side' and 'Queen's Side' apartments to the east and west respectively. These progressed from 'public' Presence Chambers on the north front round to 'private' bedchambers overlooking the park, although the King's side would never really be used as such. In May 1662 Charles also asked André Le Nôtre, creator of the gardens at Versailles for Louis XIV, to produce a parterre garden design for the park to the south of the House, probably incorporating work he had already started, including 'giant steps' down what is now the Observatory hill (Castle Hill) completed that April. One idea was to include a cascade of water down the hill, but this and Le Nôtre's other detailed suggestions never progressed. Time has softened the 17th-century park landscape but its layout of tree avenues remains intact.

Henrietta Maria landed at Greenwich from France in July 1662 and briefly resumed occupation of the House while Somerset House (her former London residence) was adapted for her. Perhaps hastened by sad memories, her move there in September (before Somerset House was completed) ended the history of Greenwich as a 'royal seat'. The Queen's House remained vested in successive queens but saw only occasional royal visits or overnight stays, usually related to Greenwich's role as the ceremonial hub of important arrivals and departures by royal yacht for the Continent.

Grace and favour

By the end of the 17th century, the Queen's House had slipped into new 'grace-and-favour' uses, made available to those whom royalty wished to favour or reward. One of Charles II's mistresses, Jane Middleton, lodged there, and for about 20 years from the winter of 1672/3 Willem van de Velde the Elder and the Younger, the Dutch father and son who introduced marine painting to England under Charles II's patronage, had their studio in the House (see page 22).

In 1675–76, the first Astronomer Royal, John Flamsteed, lived in and observed from the House while his new Observatory was built on the hill above. The Marquis de Rouvigny, a French Huguenot (Calvinist Protestant) refugee, and former French ambassador to Charles II, was a longer-term tenant by 1686. He shared quarters for a time with another French exile, the traveller Sir John Chardin, by then jeweller to the English court. At this point, one room of the House was used as a Huguenot chapel, with services in French for other Huguenots living locally.

▼ The Royal Observatory from Crooms Hill, *English school, about 1696. The Queen's House can be seen in the background.*

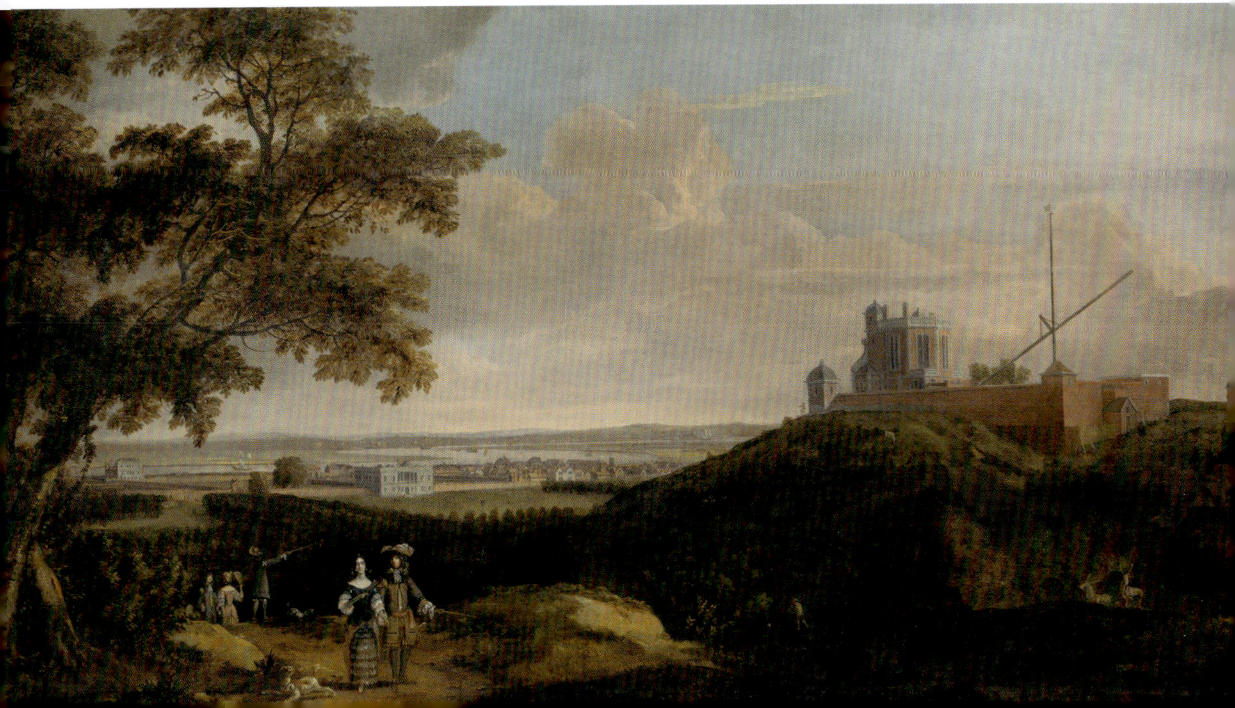

The Willem van de Veldes

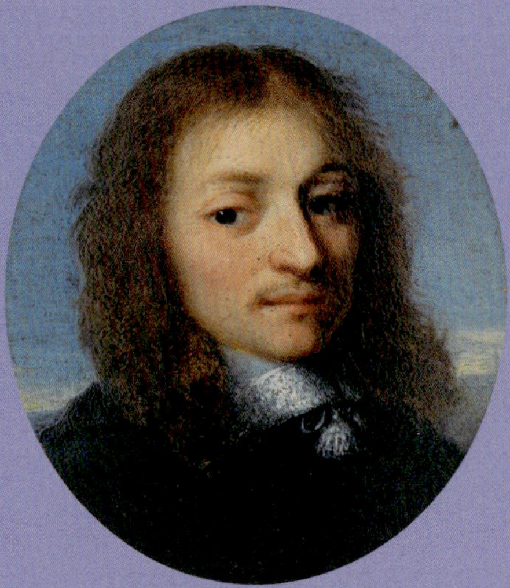

▲ Willem van de Velde the Younger (1633–1707), *artist unknown, about 1675–76.*

The Willem van de Veldes were the most sought-after artists in their genre, with an impressive clientele throughout Europe. They enjoyed an extremely successful studio practice in the wealthy Dutch Republic during the mid-century but an economic downturn, combined with a general invitation to Dutch artists from Charles II, prompted them to migrate to England in the winter of 1672/3. Charles II was very fond of marine painting, and he is credited with introducing the genre to Britain. However, it was the work (and business model) of the Van de Veldes that established the local market for it, beginning a longstanding love affair among British collectors. Charles II gave the Van de Veldes use of the House's South-West Parlour as a studio and paid each £100 a year: the father for drawing 'sea fights' and the son for 'putting the said Draughts into colours'. They were also allowed space on the upper floor to lay out the enormous cartoons (full-size preparatory drawings) required to fulfil a commission from James, Duke of York, for a series of tapestries depicting the Battle of Solebay (1672). The National Maritime Museum holds the world's largest collection of works by the Van de Veldes, including one of the Solebay weavings: the others in the set belong to the Royal Collection and Historic Royal Palaces.

Van de Velde the Elder (1611–93) was primarily a draughtsman, and a master of the grisaille 'pen painting' technique, using fine lines and cross-hatching to produce exquisitely detailed monochrome images on a special white-painted ground. His work provides an exceptional record of 17th-century ships and seafaring, and also delights in anecdotal detail. Van de Velde the Younger (1633–1707), originally his father's pupil, was also a natural draughtsman, but a better painter in oils, where his talent for rendering the effects of light on the watery world were put to best use.

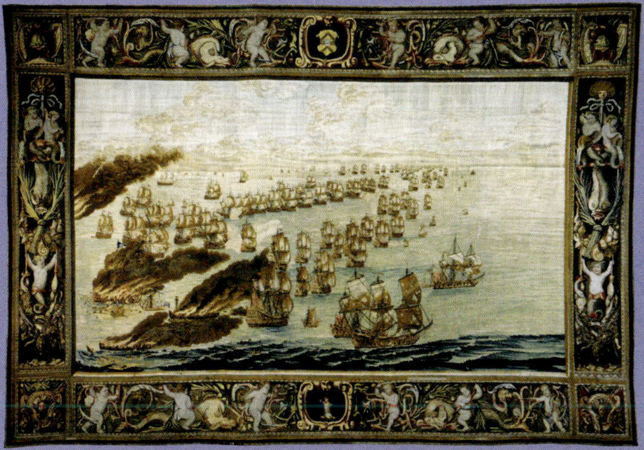

Mortlake Tapestry, *Thomas Poyntz, about 1672. One of the six Solebay tapestries woven after designs by William van de Velde the Elder.*

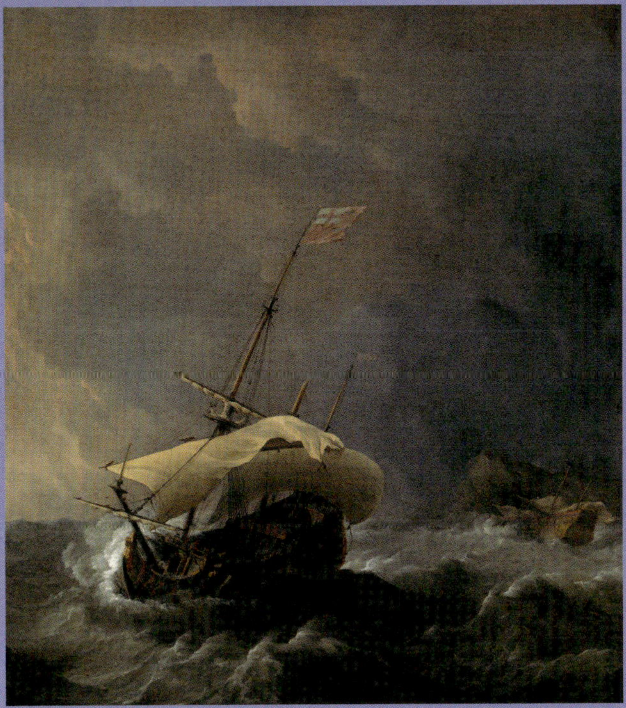

An English ship in a gale trying to claw off a lee shore, *Willem van de Velde the Younger, 1672. Signed 'London, 1672' this is one of the first pictures painted by the Van de Veldes in England.*

The Queen's House under the Rangers

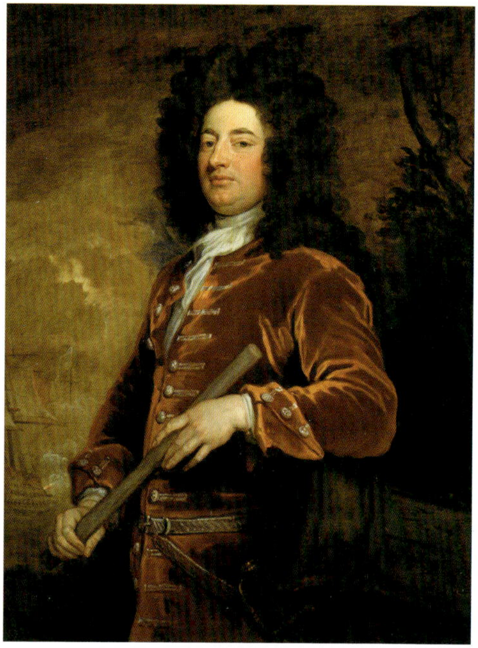

▲ Admiral Sir John Jennings (1664–1743), *Sir Godfrey Kneller, 1708–09.*

From 1690 the House was attached to the new post of Ranger of Greenwich Park, an honorary position in the gift of the Crown. In 1697, the post passed to Henry, Earl of Romney, who quickly redirected the public road that ran under the House, moving it north to its present position (as the modern Romney Road, between the Queen's House and the Old Royal Naval College). This diversion of the road made it possible to insert new rooms linking the north and south sides of the house at ground level; the first had been built under the Central Bridge by 1710.

In 1714, the Elector of Hanover, who became George I, landed at Greenwich and spent his first night in his new kingdom at the Queen's House. It was also here in 1736 that his son Prince Frederick (father of George III) welcomed his bride Augusta of Saxe-Gotha to England. During this time the House was used as the residence of the Governor of Greenwich Hospital, who doubled as Park Ranger, while construction of the Hospital continued on the palace site. Its longest serving Governor, Admiral Sir John Jennings, was resident for 23 years until his death in the House in 1743, after which the official residence of the Governor was moved to the new Hospital site.

Jennings's residence at the Queen's House was surpassed in length only by that of his successor in the post of Ranger of the Park (now no longer combined with that of Governor), the formidable Lady Katharine Pelham, wife of the Prime Minister, Henry Pelham. An influential manipulator of political patronage in her own right, Lady Katharine continued as Ranger after being widowed in 1754, right up until her death in 1780, making her 37-year personal tenancy of the Queen's House the longest in its history. For such an important member of 18th-century society, it is extraordinary that there is no known portrait of Lady Katharine. Similarly, for such a long tenancy as chatelaine of the Queen's House, we know frustratingly little about how Lady Katharine used it, save for the fact that in 1745 the substantial sum of £3,000 was spent on it for her, with another £1,700 spent by 1747, and that during her tenure the central roadway was fully enclosed at ground level. As Lady Katharine also had a fine London home, the Queen's House, variously called 'Ranger's House' and 'Pelham House' during this period, presumably functioned more as a summer villa.

By 1792, the caretakers then in neglectful charge of the House were reputedly using it as the centre of a smuggling ring, but in 1795 it was fit for Caroline of Brunswick's official welcome to England for her (disastrous) marriage to George, Prince of Wales, later George IV. On disembarking to a reception including massed ranks of Greenwich Pensioners, she was reputedly overheard to remark (in French), 'Are all Englishmen missing an arm or a leg?'

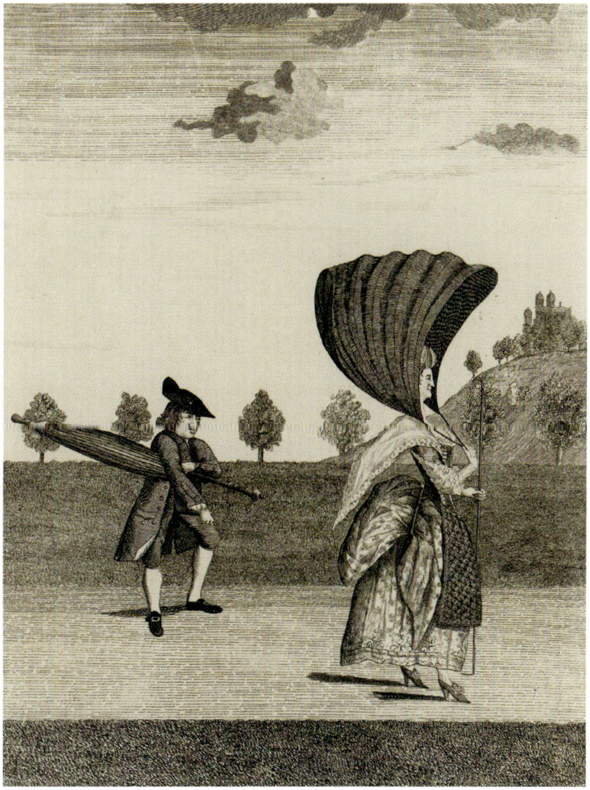

The Ton at Greenwich. A la Festoon dans le Park a Greenwich, *Darly, 1777. The primary figure in this caricature is unidentified but there is a possibility that it could be Lady Katharine.*

School days

In 1806, separated from her husband and living at Montagu House, Blackheath, on the south-west corner of Greenwich Park, Princess Caroline was appointed Ranger, a position she held until 1814. She never took up residence in the Queen's House, however, after an official costing exercise proposed that it instead become the new home of the Royal Naval Asylum, an orphanage school for the children of naval seamen, which had been established in Paddington in 1798. Caroline accepted £7,875 to remain at Montagu House and after it was demolished in 1815, the late-17th-century Brunswick House (formerly Chesterfield House) became the official residence of the Ranger. It is still called Ranger's House today although the last Ranger (Lord Garnet Woleseley) left in 1890.

▼ *Early school photograph, about 1850–55.*

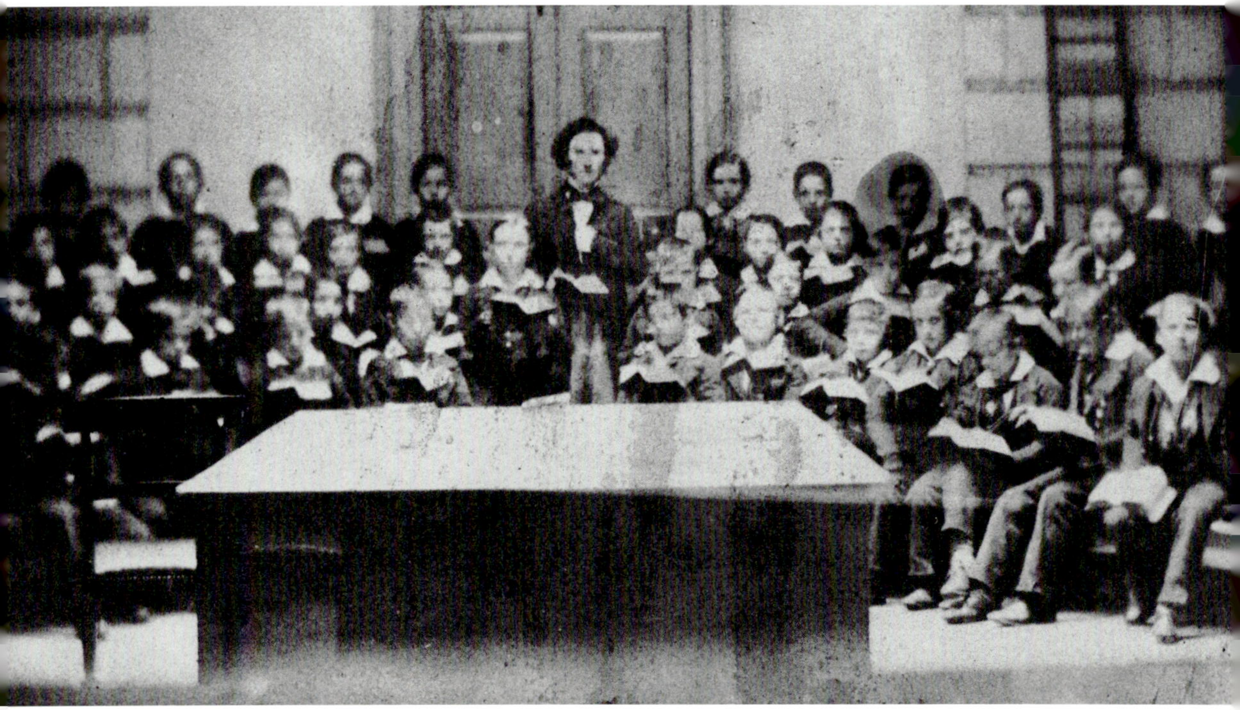

Asylum staff and the first 70 girls took up residence in the Queen's House in November 1807, but it was not large enough for the whole school. To meet the need for additional accommodation, the architect Daniel Asher Alexander designed separate east and west wings – connected to the House by colonnades – which were completed in 1809. These wings were further extended to the north by 1811.

From 1821 – but only formally from 1825 – the Asylum was combined, under Greenwich Hospital, with the Hospital school for the sons of seamen (which had been founded around 1712–15). The Asylum intake became the junior or 'Lower School' and, until 1841, the House, or 'Centre Building', as it became known, provided quarters for up to 200 girls, who had a segregated walled garden area to the north. They trained for domestic service and the boys – occupying the wings – for careers at sea. In 1841, which also saw pupil disturbances that prompted rapid educational reforms, girls' schooling ended and the House was further altered to become mainly staff apartments, with some teaching spaces. The School had two roof-lit ground-level classrooms in the open wells between the top-floor bridges by 1875, the eastern one housed a school 'museum'. What this held is unknown, but a letter from the British Museum in August 1853 frostily declined a School request for 'any objects of interest they can spare' to populate it. A staff garden on the south side was separated from the park by a low wall and ditch to keep the park deer out, and railings between the columns forming the south-side of the colonnade kept the children out. The colonnades provided sheltered play space, which eventually looked out over a huge asphalt parade ground to the north. From 1843, the first of three full-size, fully rigged 'model ships' stood in front of the House. On these the boys learnt the art of seamanship under sail as well as the discipline and courage required for working aloft. The last of the ships, called *Fame*, was built in 1873.

Vocational, technical and regimented, by the 1850s the School was highly regarded and its output ably self-reliant. The elite navigational students of the Upper School were routinely placed in training posts in Royal Navy ships, many becoming commissioned officers, including a few admirals. In 1892, Queen Victoria recognised its achievements: hitherto the 'Greenwich Hospital Schools', it became instead the 'Royal Hospital School'. The First World War took the lives of 151 former pupils who had attended the school between 1889 and 1918. The youngest was 14.

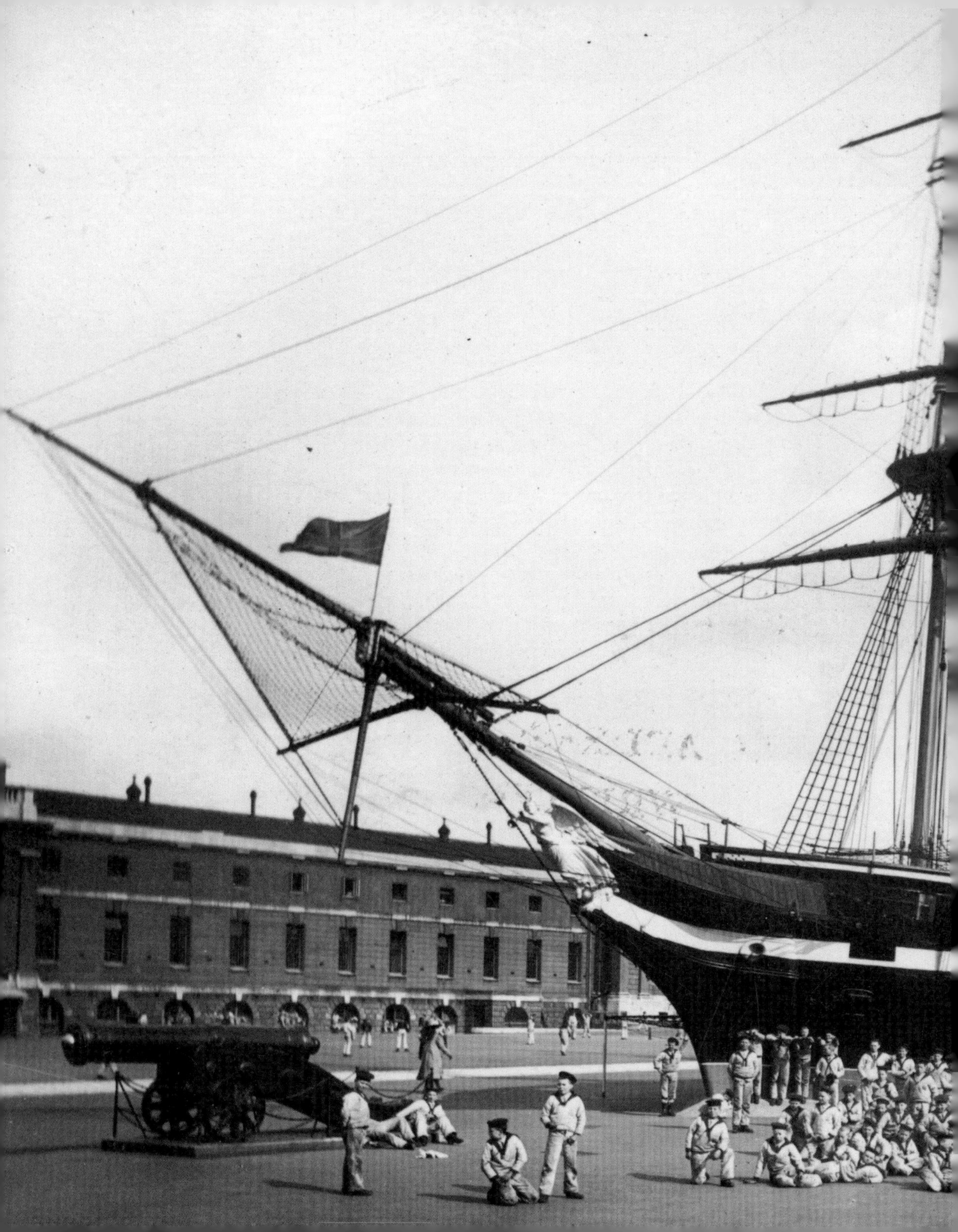

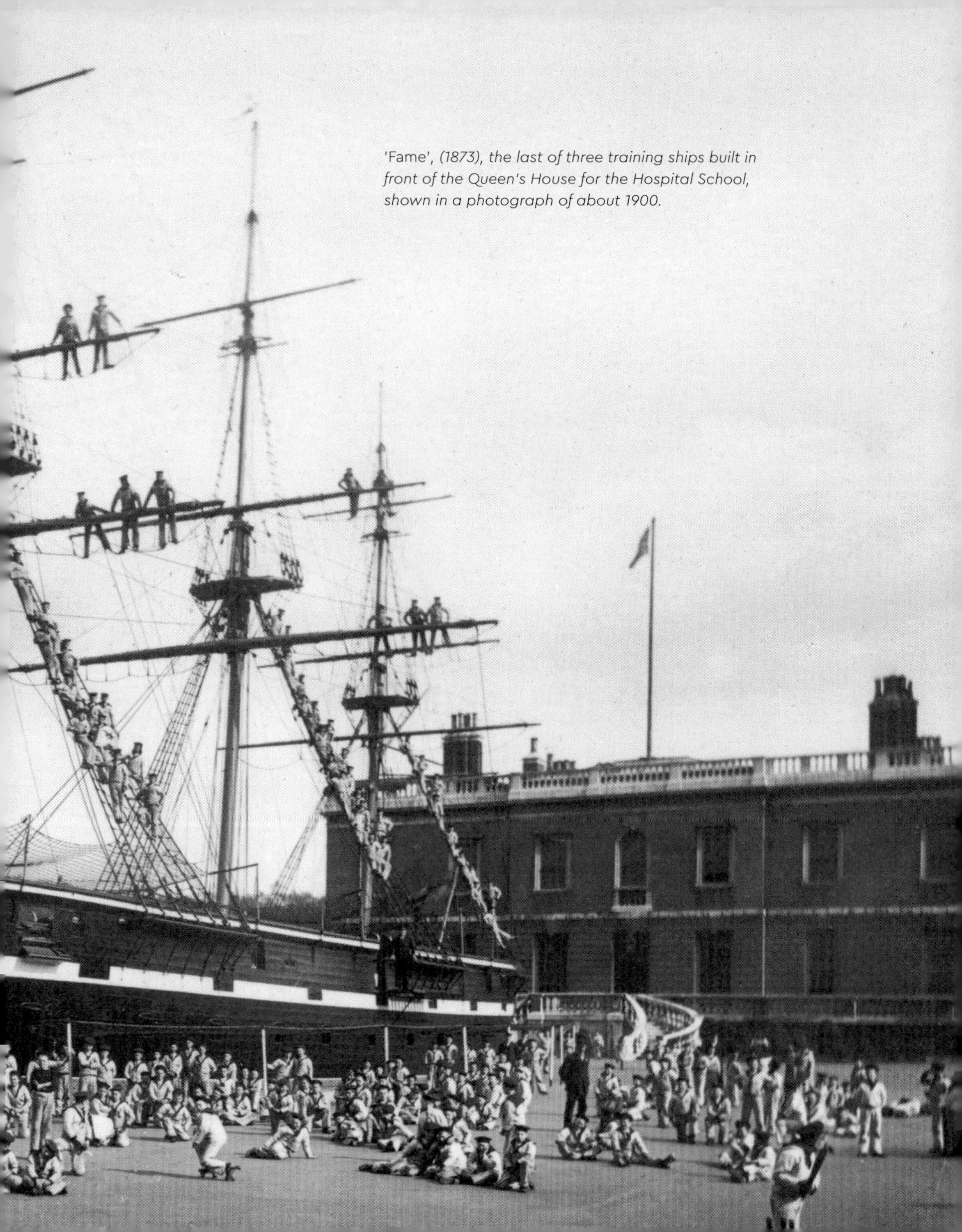

'Fame', (1873), the last of three training ships built in front of the Queen's House for the Hospital School, shown in a photograph of about 1900.

The National Maritime Museum

Plans for a 'national naval and nautical museum' at Greenwich were underway from the late 1920s. They coincided with the proposed relocation of the Royal Hospital School to Suffolk, which eventually took place when new buildings were complete in 1933. Proposals to use the Queen's House as the home of the new museum were initially met with resistance from the Office of Works, which had intended to refurbish and open it to the public as a stately home, and was concerned that its architectural significance would become subordinate to 'museum specimens'. Ultimately it was the plan for a museum that prevailed: the House was to become 'a People's Palace of British Sea-Power', in the words of the then Chairman of the Society for Nautical Research. The Office of Works then embarked on an extensive project with the aim of restoring it to its 17th-century state, or at least to the greatest extent possible given all that the fabric had endured in the

▼ *King George VI speaking in Neptune Hall during the formal opening of the National Maritime Museum, 27 April 1937. Seated on either side of the King are Princess Elizabeth, Queen Elizabeth and Queen Mary. In the background is a tapestry designed in the Queen's House by Willem van de Velde the Elder (see p. 23).*

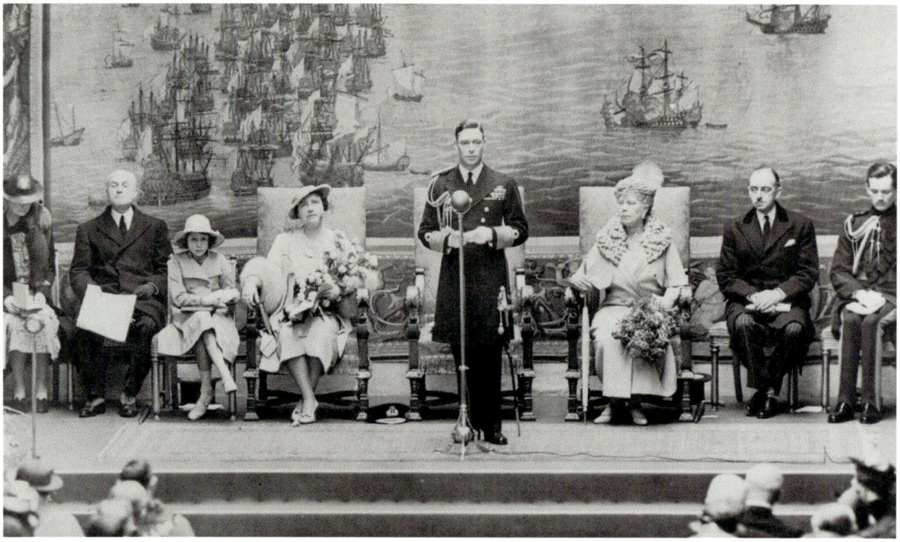

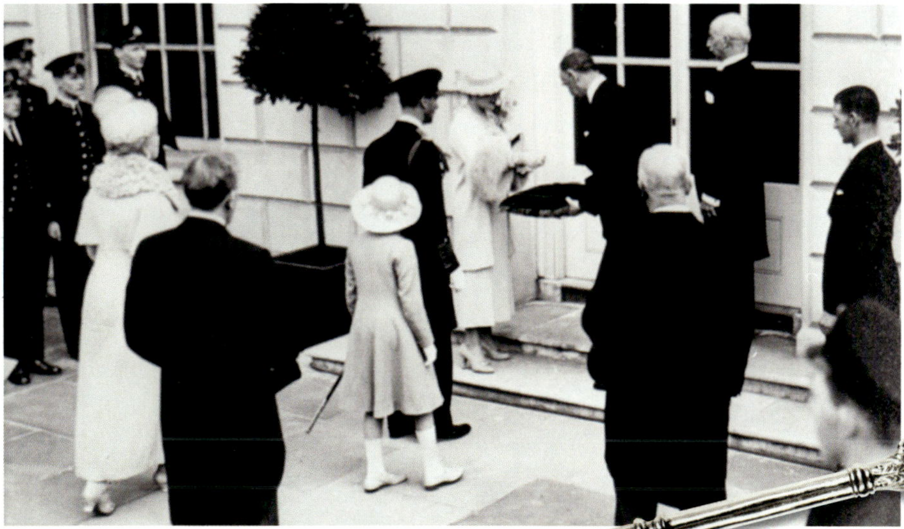

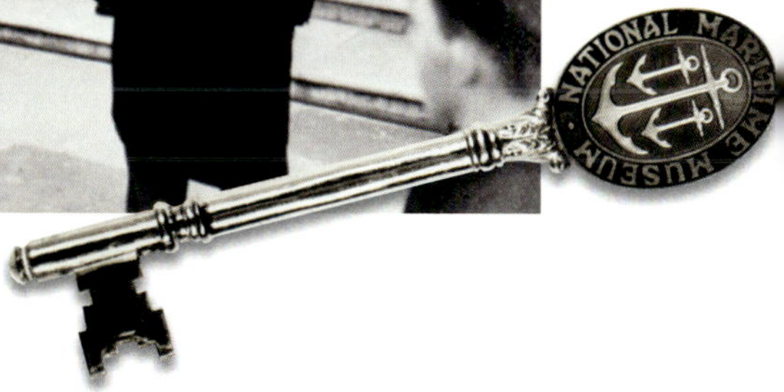

▲ ▶ *Queen Elizabeth uses a special golden key to open the door to the Great Hall, 27 April 1937.*

intervening centuries. The inspector of works, George Chettle, who also wrote the first authoritative study of the House's architecture and history, led the work. The most striking external change was the demolition of the rooms that had blocked the central roadway since about 1708, opening up the full east-west vista along the later colonnades for the first time.

On 27 April 1937, King George VI, Queen Elizabeth and their elder daughter Princess Elizabeth sailed in the motor launch *Nore* from Westminster Pier to Greenwich to open the new National Maritime Museum. By then the Museum footprint had expanded beyond the Queen's House to include what are now the Museum buildings to west and east. Three weeks before the coronation, the opening of the Museum was the first major public event of the new King's reign and was stage-managed as an opportunity for his subjects to acclaim his unexpected succession to his brother, Edward VIII, whose abdication in 1936 had caused a national crisis. On the north terrace of the Queen's House, Queen Elizabeth unlocked the door to its Great Hall with a special golden key and so began a new phase in the life of a building completed 300 years earlier for very different purposes.

The interiors of the House were then rather spartan: plain off-white walls displayed portraits and marine paintings, with some glass-cased ship models and other exhibits telling the early story of Britain's rise to seaborne Empire under the Tudors and Stuarts, and of 'old Greenwich'. These chronologically arranged displays were continued in the Caird Galleries of the building to the west of the House, today's National Maritime Museum.

The Museum had been open to visitors for hardly two years when the

▼ *The Duchess of Kent inspects a unit of the Women's Royal Naval Service ('Wrens') outside the National Maritime Museum, 27 January 1944.*

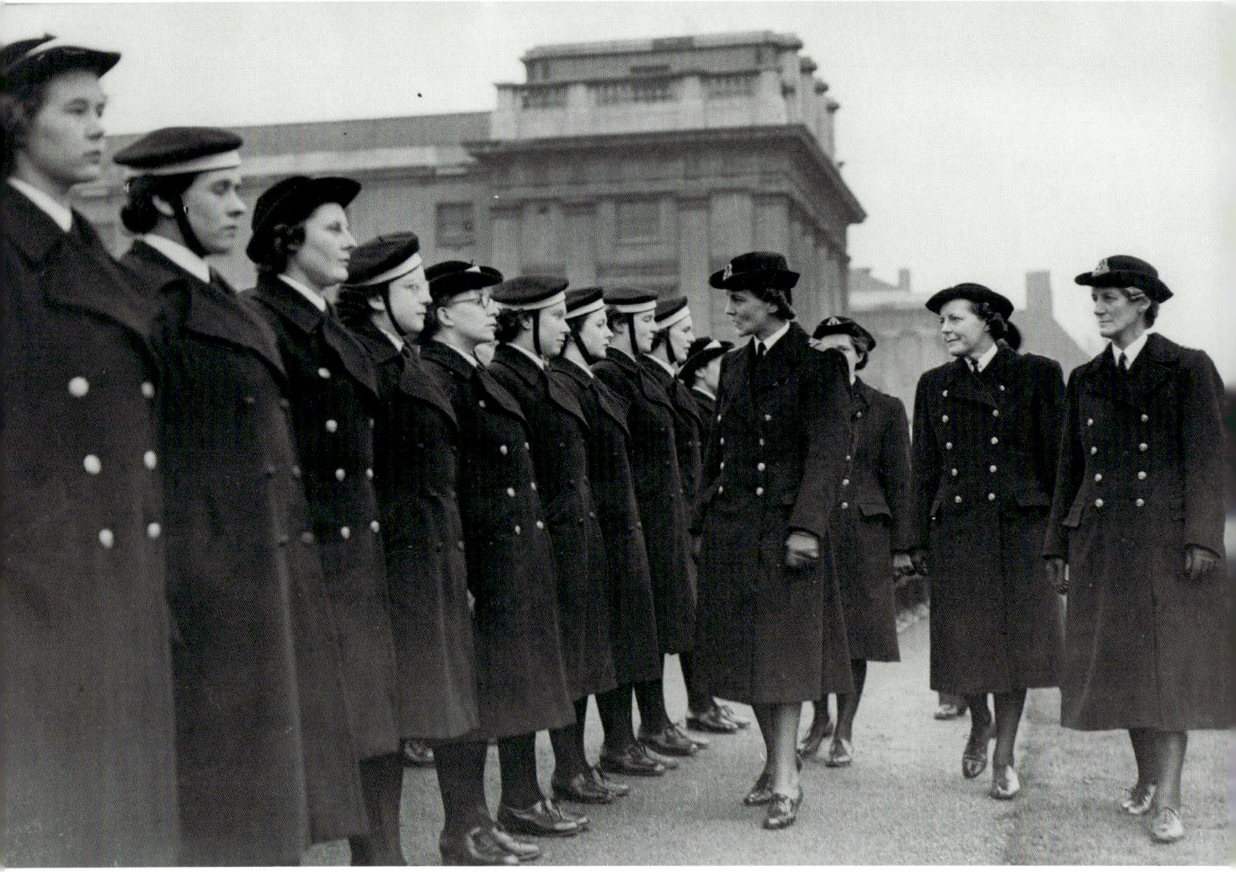

Second World War broke out. An air-raid shelter was built in the basement of the Queen's House and in 1941 the entire House was requisitioned by the Admiralty for naval use. Once again it became a residence, this time housing a detachment of the Women's Royal Naval Service ('Wrens'). The Museum's treasures were removed for safekeeping, with only a morale-boosting display in the Great Hall remaining. The Queen's House was extremely lucky to escape destruction in an area that was otherwise badly damaged both by bombing raids and by V-1 and V-2 rockets: blast damage from near-misses was fortunately slight, and an incendiary-bomb fire in the roof was quickly put out. After the war, the House opened its doors to the public again in April 1947, though it was not until late 1949 that all the necessary repairs had been completed and the collection fully reinstalled.

'House of Delight' for the 21st century

The Queen's House remains the 'jewel in the crown' of Royal Museums Greenwich, and the park-and-palace landscape of the Maritime Greenwich World Heritage Site – so-inscribed by UNESCO in 1997.

Successive redisplays every couple of decades over the course of the second half of the 20th century have taken different approaches to the unique challenges presented by the House, reconciling its extraordinary architectural importance with a superb art collection, particularly strong in marine painting and portraiture. Most recently, in 2016, a major refurbishment and redisplay project saw the House presented afresh in a manner that is both aesthetically led and historically based. If visitors to the Queen's House today are sometimes surprised by the absence of reconstructed 'period rooms' attempting to create a literal evocation of the 17th-century royal villa, they should not be disappointed by an approach that instead, and for our own times, seeks to evoke the spirit of the House, as originally intended by its 17th-century royal patrons. In the 1630s the House gleamed against the historical buildings of Tudor Greenwich and was filled by Henrietta Maria with contemporary art. Today the works of both old masters, such as the Van de Veldes, and highly regarded contemporary artists, such as Richard Wright and Kehinde Wiley, fill the same finely proportioned rooms and prompt visitors to think about their place in the long history and tradition that the House and its collections encompass.

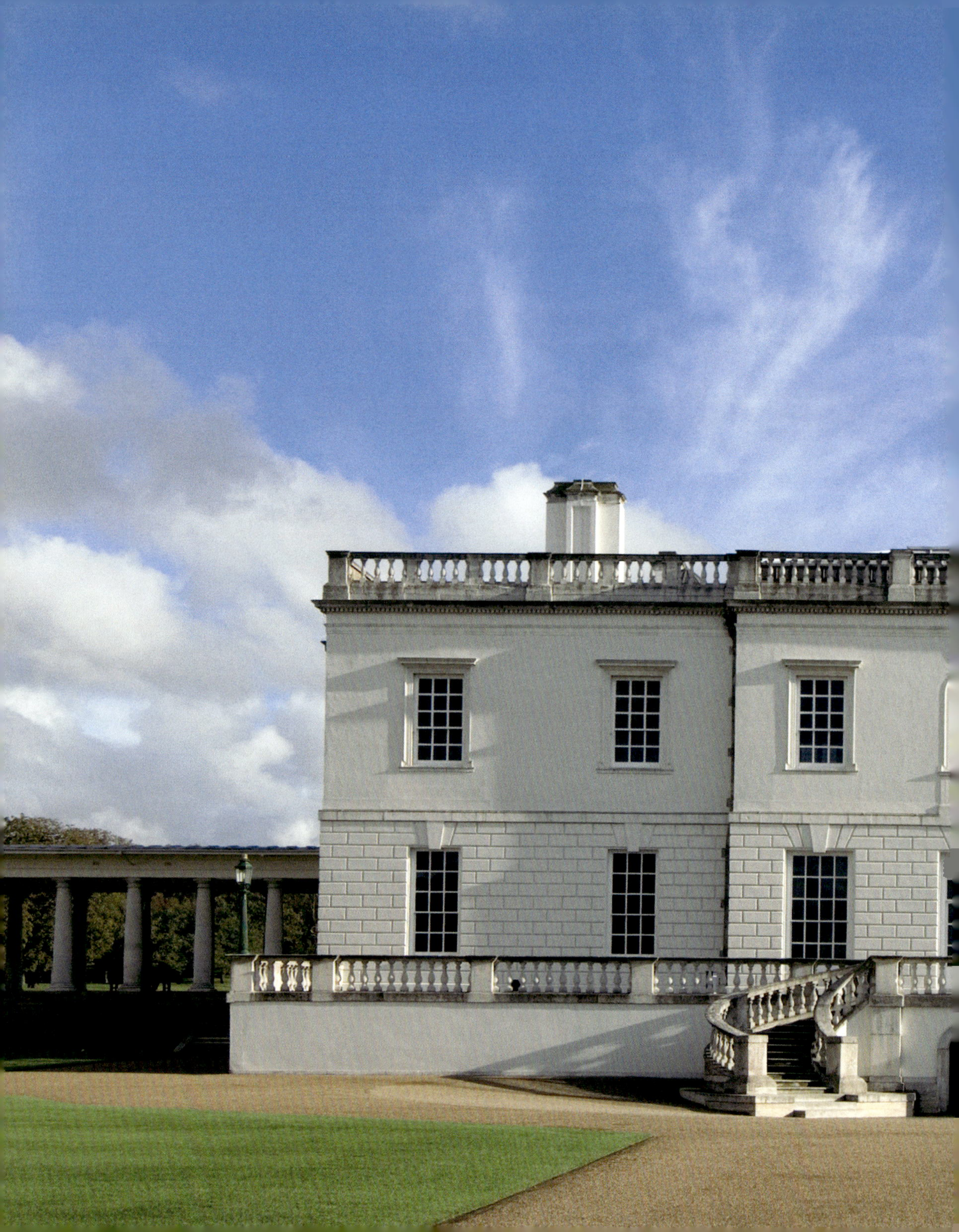

Architecture and interior

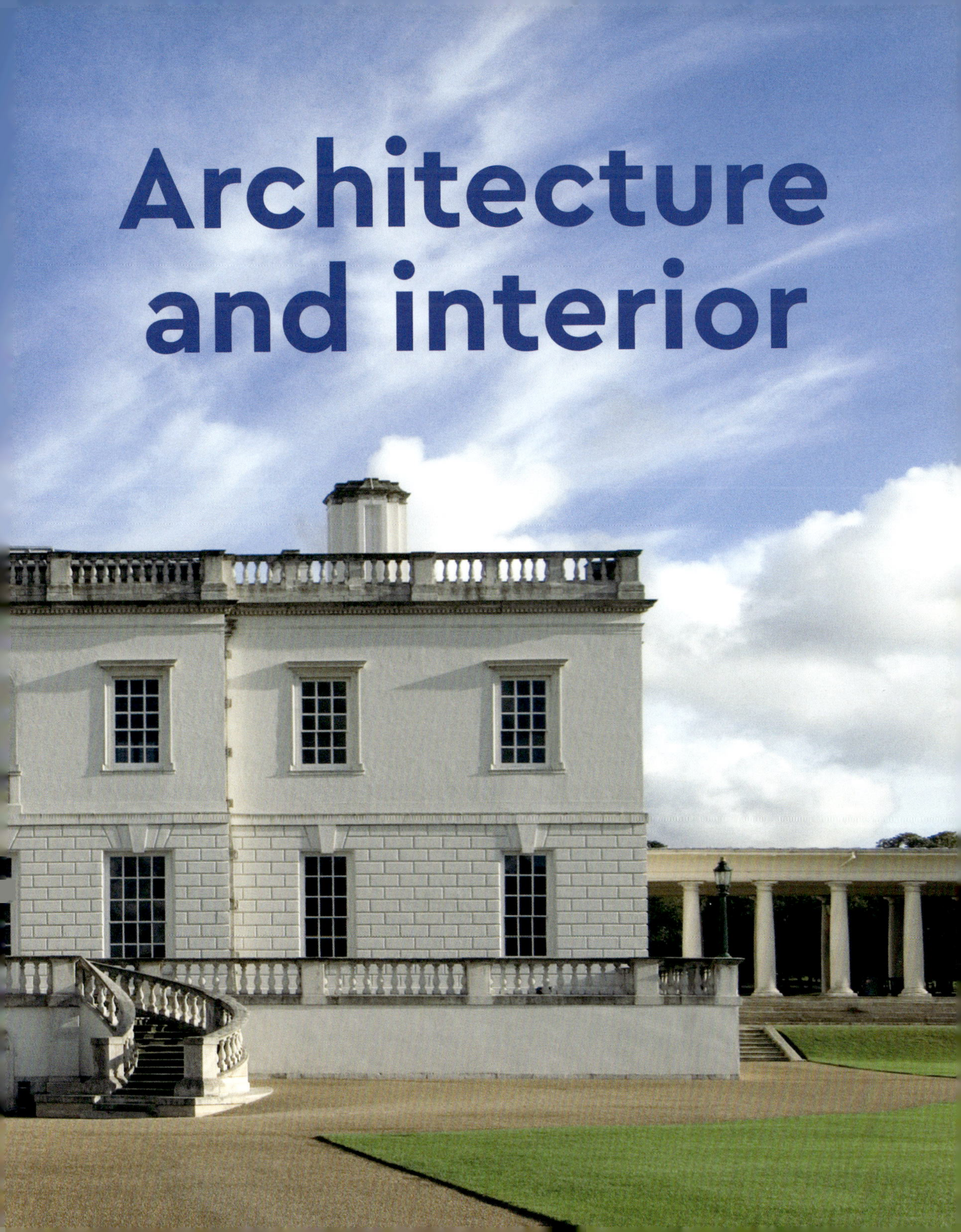

Style and exterior

Designed by Inigo Jones in 1616 and completed in about 1638, the Queen's House is of unique significance as the first building in England constructed in the Italian Renaissance manner. This style is generally called 'Palladian' after the architect Andrea Palladio, whose villas Jones studied first-hand in Italy in 1613–14, shortly before he began work on the House. In 18th-century Britain this style transformed into classical 'Georgian', the dominant national style in British architecture until the mid-19th century and still influential today. The Queen's House therefore constitutes the stylistic point of origin not only of the great buildings of Greenwich that surround it, but of classical architecture in Britain more generally.

Although by the 1690s the Queen's House had become a grace-and-favour residence, not used by the monarchs themselves, it is to Mary II that the House owes its view to and from the Thames, which it did not originally have owing to the intervening bulk of the old palace. When Sir Christopher Wren designed the Old Royal Naval College (as Greenwich Hospital) for

▼ The Elevation of the Queen's House to the Park at Greenwich ..., *Colen Campbell, 1715. This image of the Queen's House was included in a publication on British architecture, although it is not thought that the roof was ever decorated with statues like the ones shown here.*

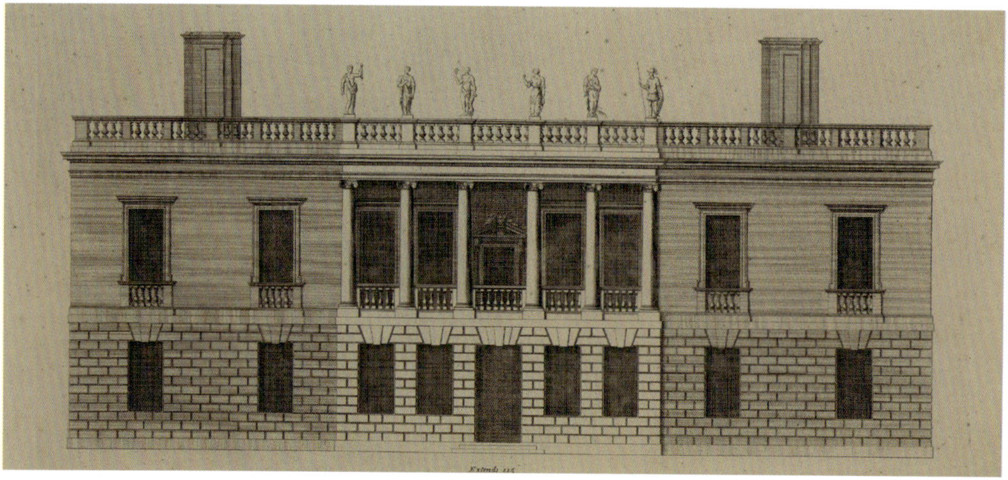

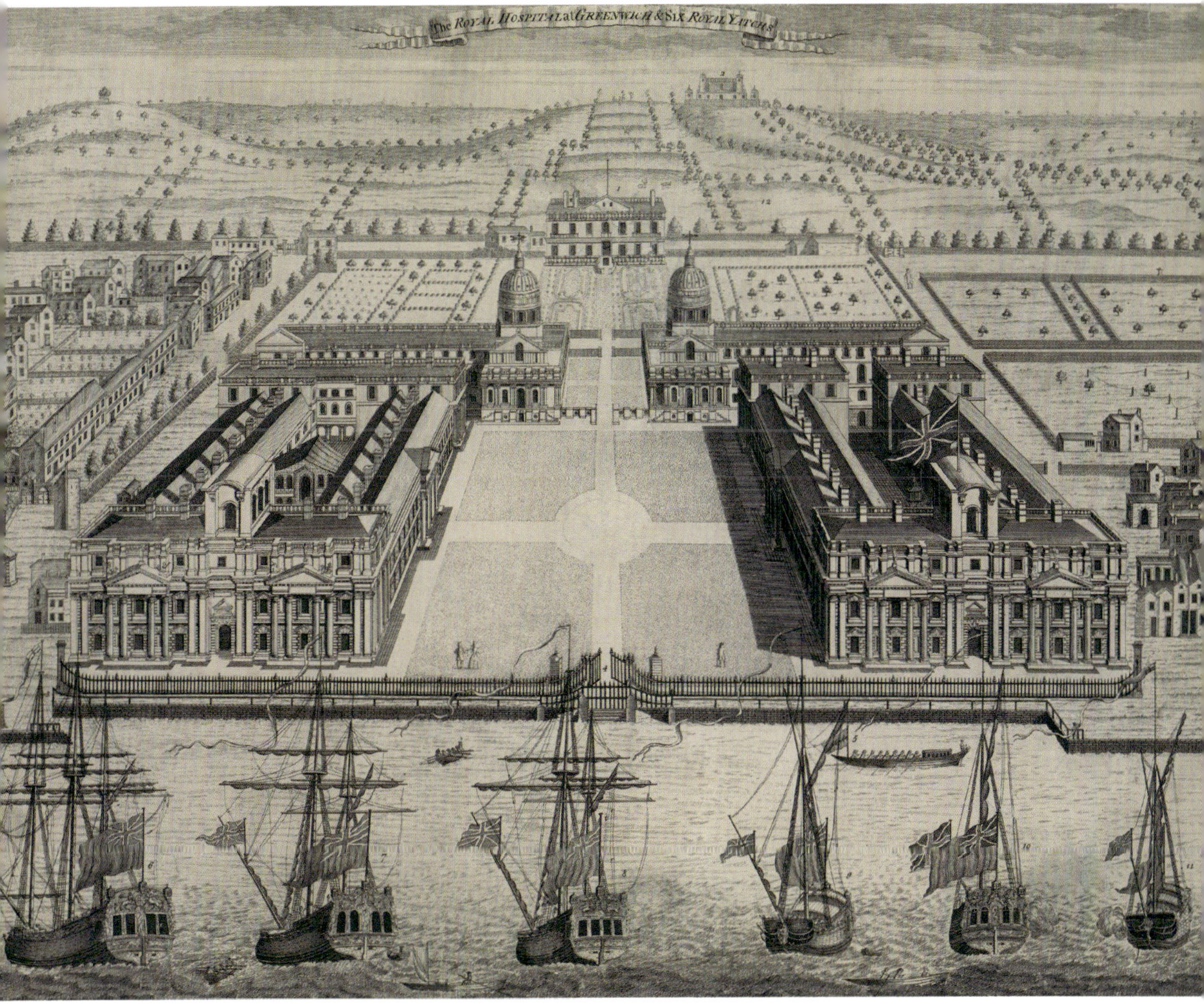

▲ The Royal Hospital at Greenwich & six royal Yatchs [sic: Yachts], *R. Olive, about 1720.*

building on the old palace site in the early 1690s, Mary, the prime champion of the project, ordered that the College should not block the new 'visto' from the Queen's House to the river. The closest distance between the College 'courts' is exactly the width of the House (35.4 metres).

Facing away from the river and towards the park, in keeping with the original ceremonial function of the building, the elegant first-floor loggia is the principal external feature of the House. In an annotation to his copy of Palladio's treatise on architecture, Inigo Jones had commented in 1615 that such 'a frontispiece in the midest' was a house's finest ornament: that on the south façade of the Queen's House is the earliest first-floor loggia known in England. Serving as an 'ornament' to focus attention was undoubtedly its royal purpose, especially given that, in the 1600s, the park was used solely by those close to the court: it only became 'public' in modern terms in the early 19th century. The Ionic columns, said to be based on a slender female form, are particularly appropriate for an architectural feature that announced the Queen's domain. The Ionic order, one of the three orders of classical architecture, is also associated with temples and other buildings dedicated to Artemis and Diana, the Greek and Roman goddesses of hunting, making it additionally appropriate for the House, since Anne of Denmark and Henrietta

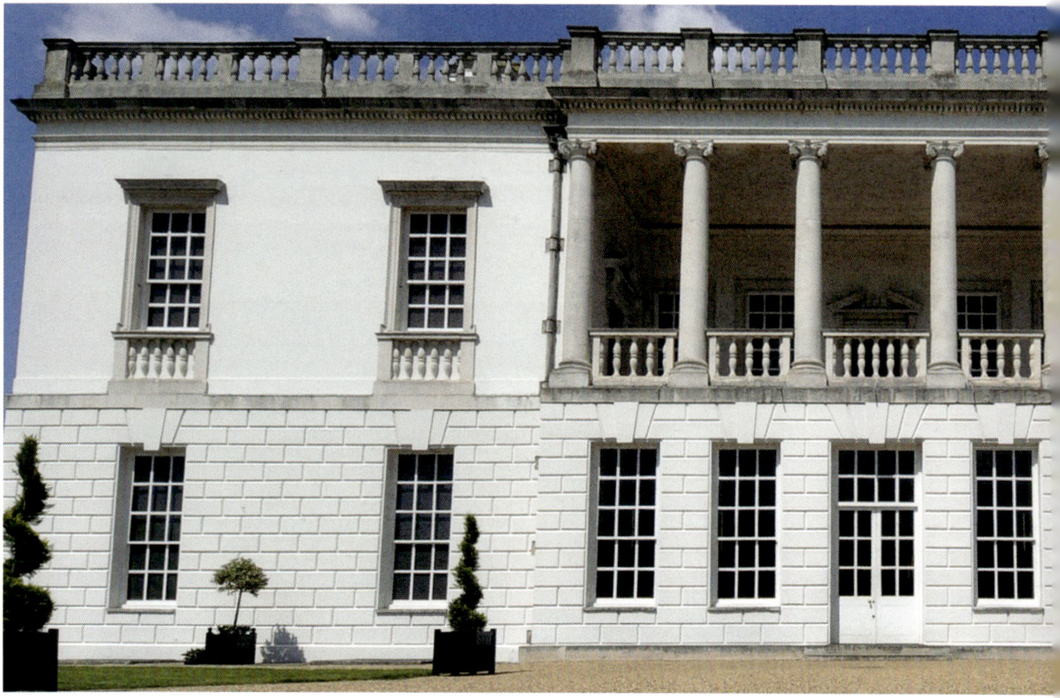

Maria were both keen huntswomen.

The terrace and 'horseshoe' stairs on the north façade (seen on page 34) were not included in Inigo Jones's original House design for Anne of Denmark. They were added after work recommenced for Henrietta Maria in 1632, shifting the architectural focus of the House towards the more private north side.

A campaign of renovations in 1708–11 saw the lower steps of the horseshoe stairs cut back and the windows updated, with Jones's original leaded-glass mullion-and-transom casements replaced by sash windows. Those on the top floor are the original dimensions; the ground-floor ones originally had higher sills but were then lengthened by cutting these down.

Set high in the north façade, above the central top-floor window, is an inscription which gives Henrietta Maria's name and title in Latin, and the date 1635. Though often stated to be the year the House was finished, that is the date of its main structural completion; substantial interior work went on until about 1638. Even then, due to the interventions of death and war, it can be said that the House was never fully finished in line with the intentions either of Anne or Henrietta Maria, nor are their full intentions for it known. Four hundred years on, that remains part of its mystery.

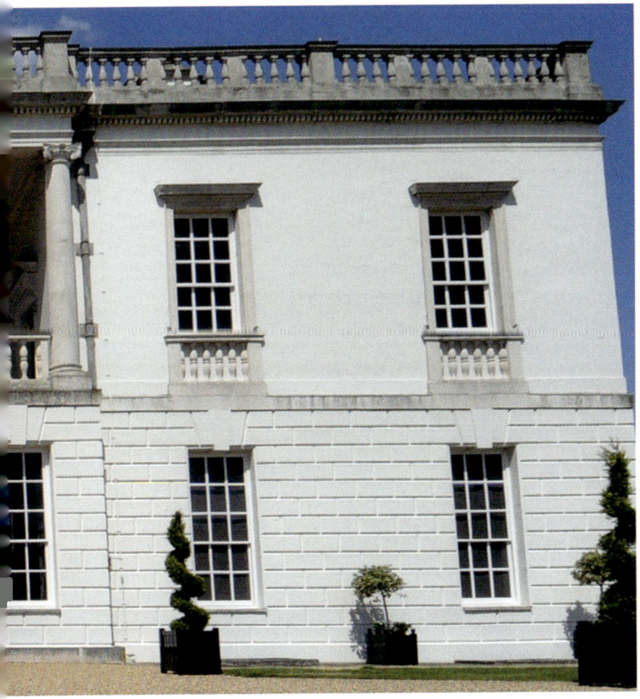

◀ *The view of the House from south showing the Loggia, a vantage point out onto Greenwich Park.*

▼ *Henrietta Maria's inscription found in the north façade.*

Greenwich and London from One Tree Hill, Johannes Vorsterman, 1680

This view of Greenwich by the Dutch artist Johannes Vorsterman was painted just after the completion of Flamsteed House, the original Royal Observatory building, in 1676. Beyond the lower park, laid for Charles II in 1661–62, fine houses run down Croom's Hill to Greenwich itself and the old Church of St Alfege (soon to be rebuilt by Hawksmoor following a roof collapse in 1710). The Queen's House, still with its original casement windows, now has its East and West Bridge Rooms, added by Charles II in the 1660s, as well as a pair of short-lived balconies which projected from them over the road below. A turret above the 'round stairs' (see Tulip Stairs on page 48) allowed enjoyment of a wide view up and down the river from the roof and, at this time still, over the

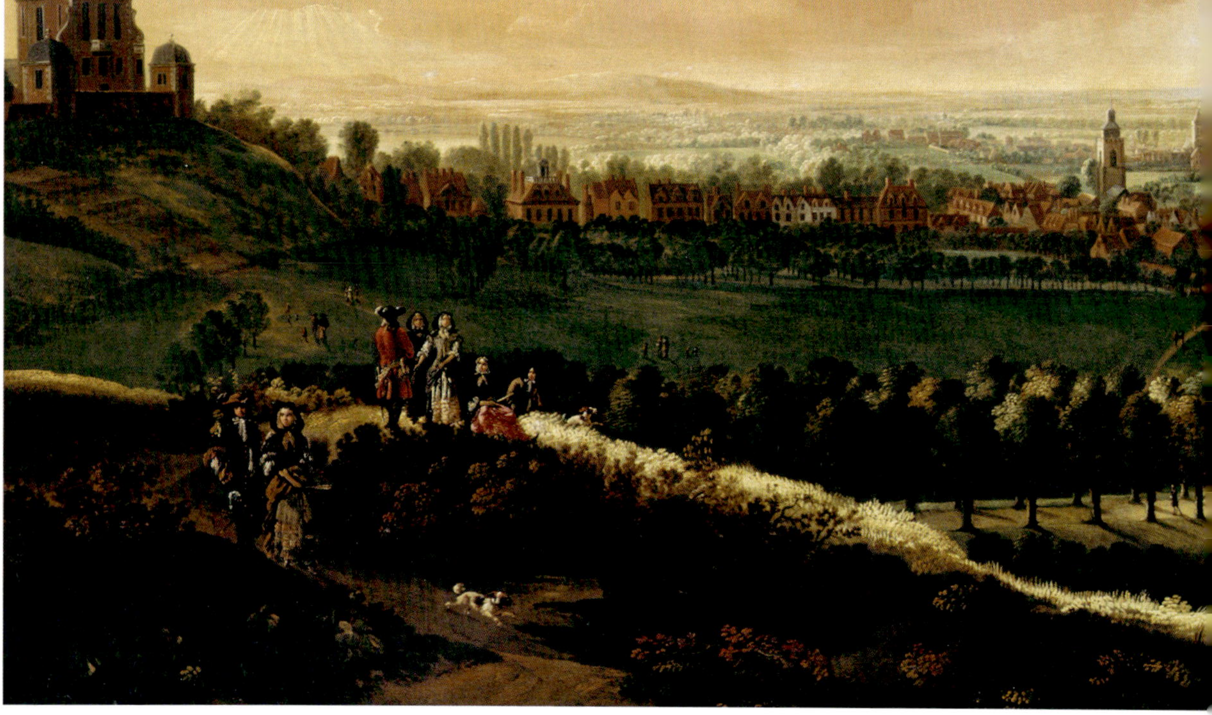

dilapidated remains of the old palace. One of the ruined towers of Henry VIII's tiltyard is obvious and less so (far right on the river edge) is the old Chapel: both of these buildings lasted into the late 1690s. The new element on the site between the Queen's House and the river is the first part of the intended 'King's House', Charles II's palace project, which had commenced in the 1660s. It remained a windowless shell until the building was incorporated from 1696 into the east front of what became the King Charles Court of Greenwich Hospital by Sir Christopher Wren. The City of London can be glimpsed in the background, including the white form of the Tower of London, while ships (including royal yachts from Deptford Dockyard) calmly make their way up and down the Thames, illustrating Greenwich's important position on the river highway.

▼ Greenwich and London from One Tree Hill, *by Johannes Vorsterman, about 1680.*

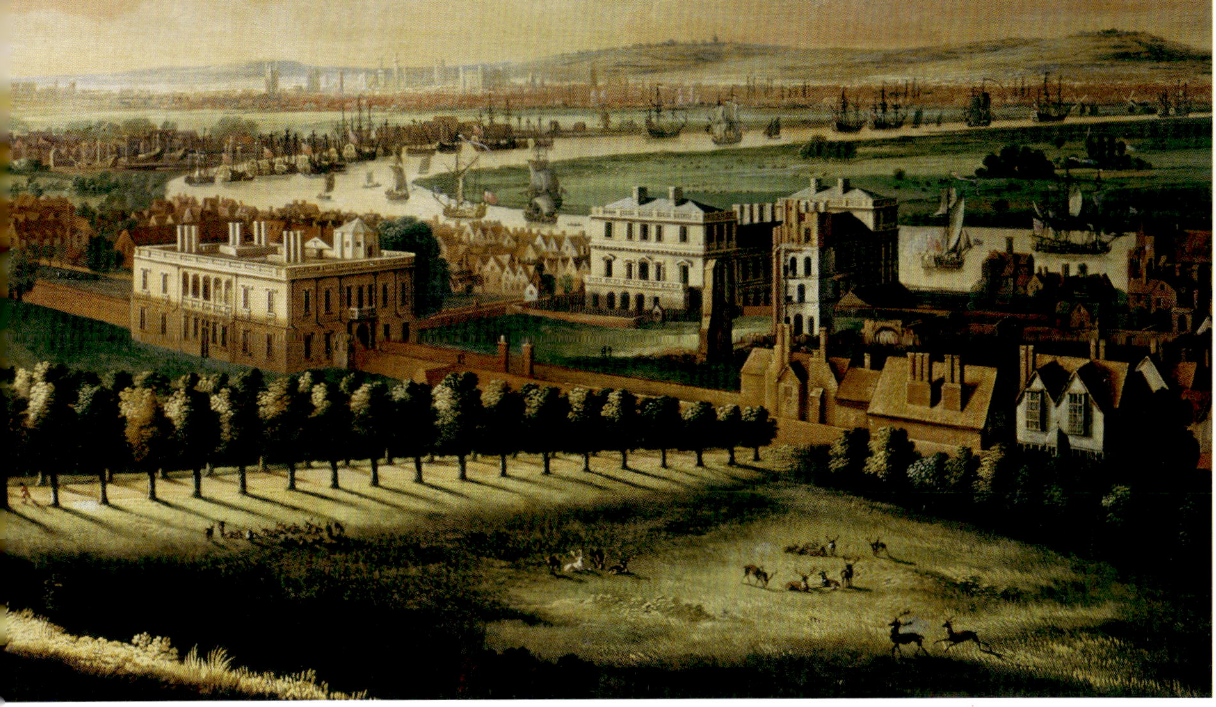

Floor plan

Ground floor

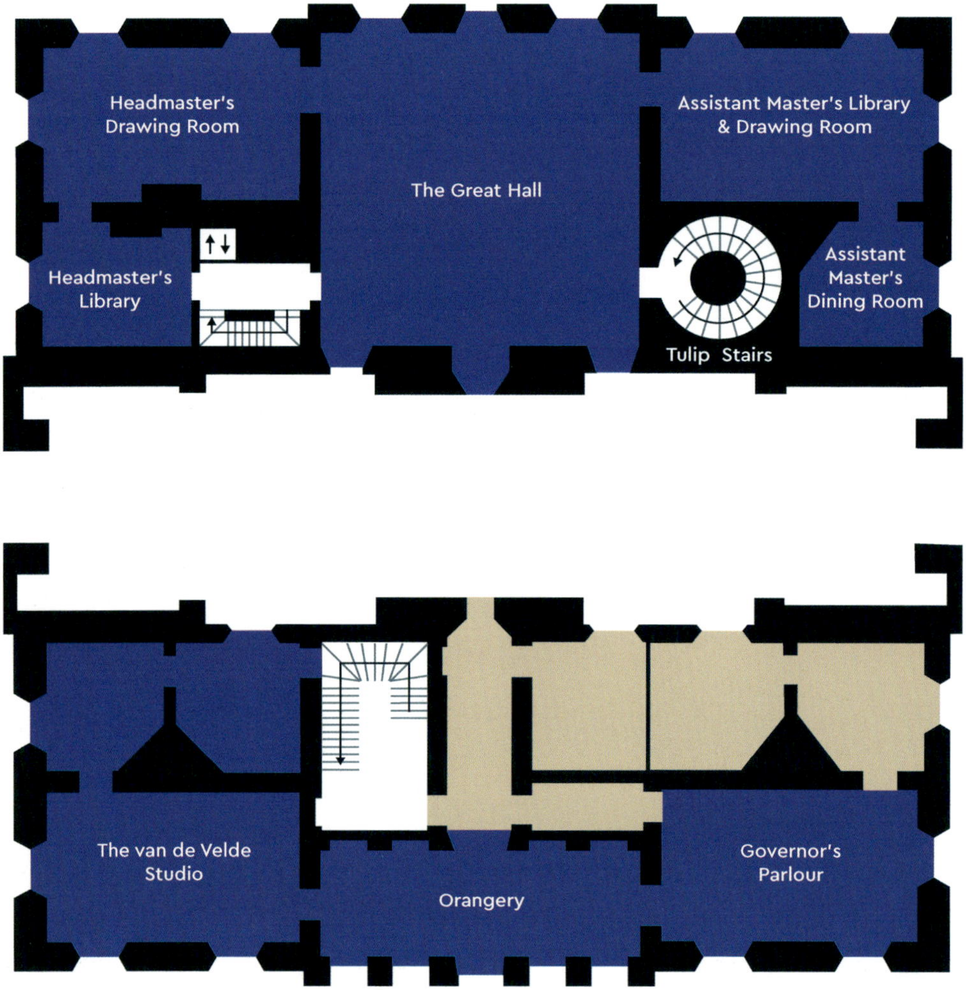

First floor

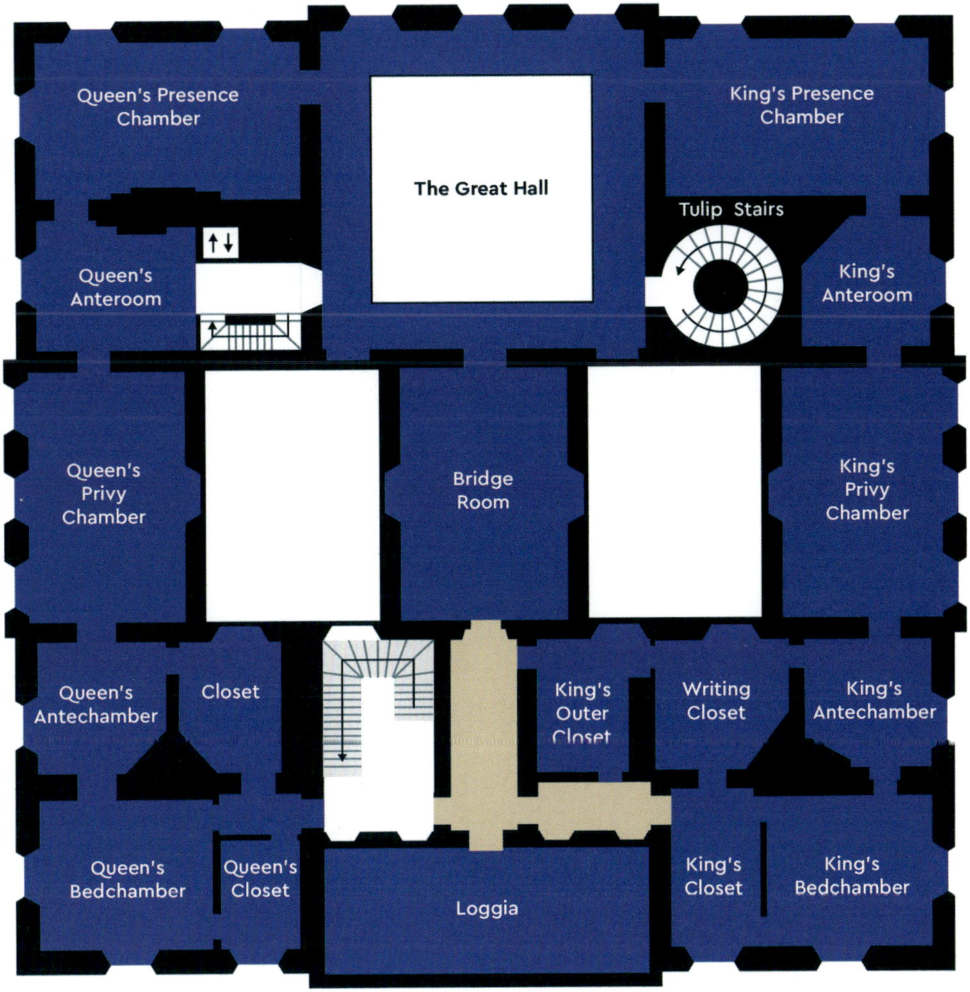
Queen's Presence Chamber
The Great Hall
King's Presence Chamber
Tulip Stairs
Queen's Anteroom
King's Anteroom
Queen's Privy Chamber
Bridge Room
King's Privy Chamber
Queen's Antechamber
Closet
King's Outer Closet
Writing Closet
King's Antechamber
Queen's Bedchamber
Queen's Closet
Loggia
King's Closet
King's Bedchamber

The Great Hall

The Great Hall was designed as a 40-foot cube, but it is not an exact one owing to construction adjustments. The floor of white Bardiglio (Italian) and black Belgian marble mirrors the formation of the ceiling compartments above. It was laid in 1636–37 under the supervision of Nicholas Stone, Charles I's Master Mason. The woodwork in the ceiling and supporting the gallery still show Inigo Jones's original paint scheme of white and gold – the colours of France – for Henrietta Maria, born a French princess: the white has degraded to the present green colour over time, under some 24 later paint layers that were finally stripped off in the 1930s refurbishment.

▼ *The Great Hall.*

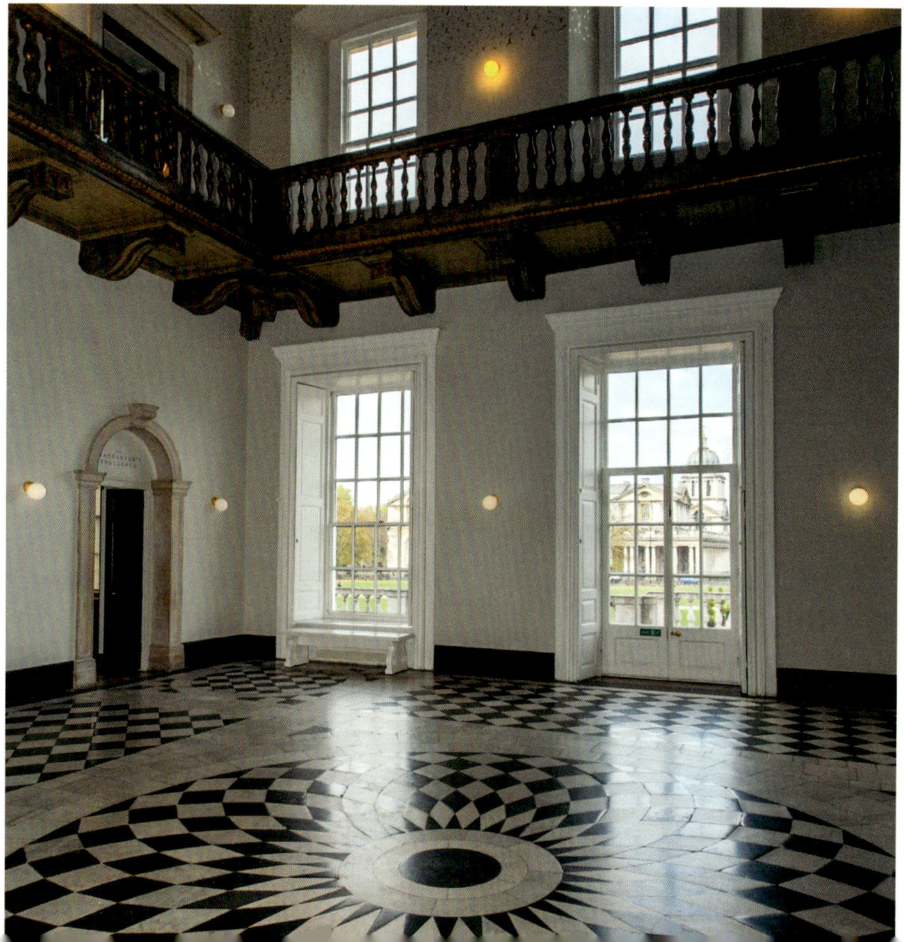

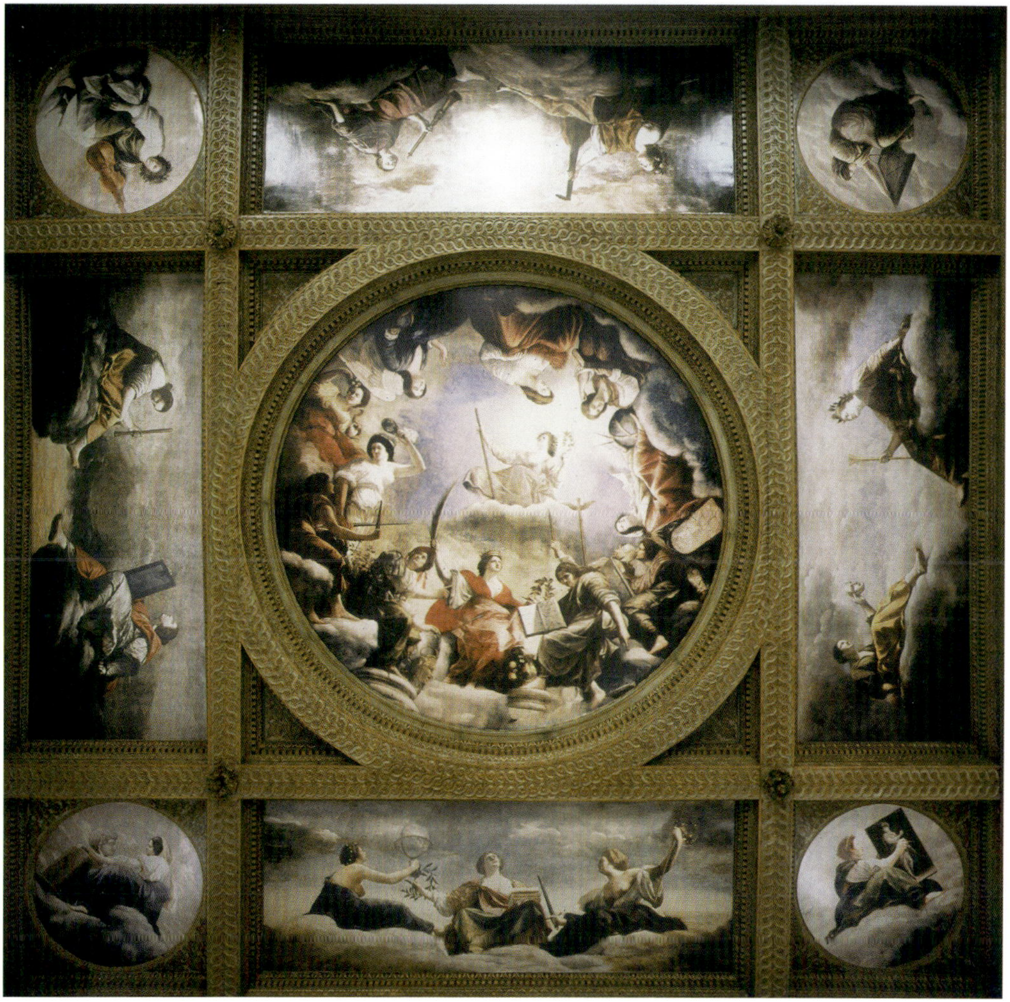

▲ *Digitally generated copy of the Gentileschi ceiling, as installed in the Great Hall during the 1990s.*

The ceiling panels were originally adorned by a suite of canvases commissioned from the Florentine painter Orazio Gentileschi, depicting 'An Allegory of Peace and the Arts under the English Crown'. The paintings were probably completed together with his daughter Artemisia, especially towards the end when his health was declining. The subject reflected Charles I and Henrietta Maria's self-image of benign and civilised rule, rendered

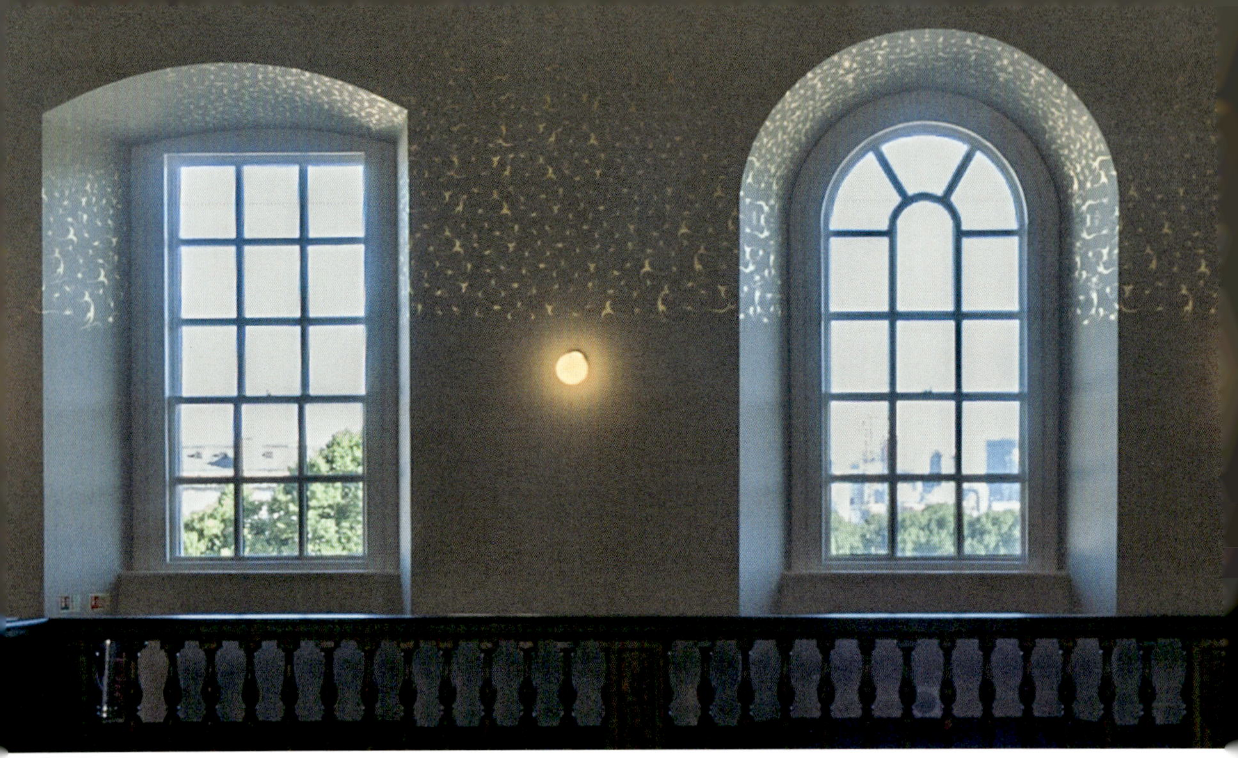

No Title, *Richard Wright*

As part of the major refurbishment of the House completed in 2016, the Turner Prize-winning artist Richard Wright was commissioned to create a work for the ceiling of the Great Hall that evoked both the splendour and the novelty of the 17th-century ceiling, originally adorned with baroque paintings. The result was a magnificent installation in gold leaf, its intricate forms inspired by those found in the hand-rail of the adjacent Tulip Stairs. Wright and his team applied the gold leaf using traditional, painstaking techniques that would have been familiar to the 17th-century craftsmen who worked on the Great Hall.

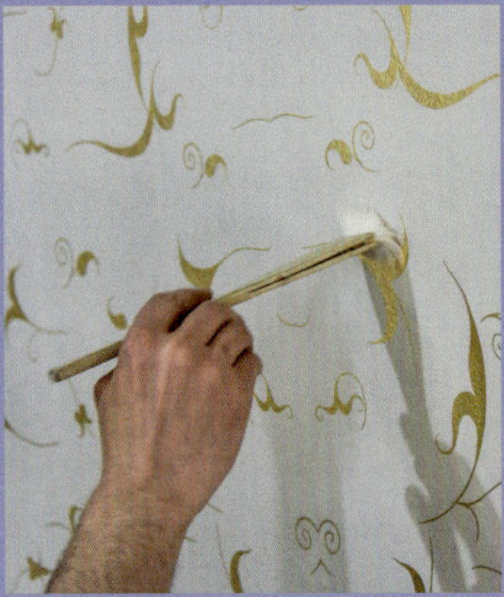

▲ *Details of the gold leaf motifs.*

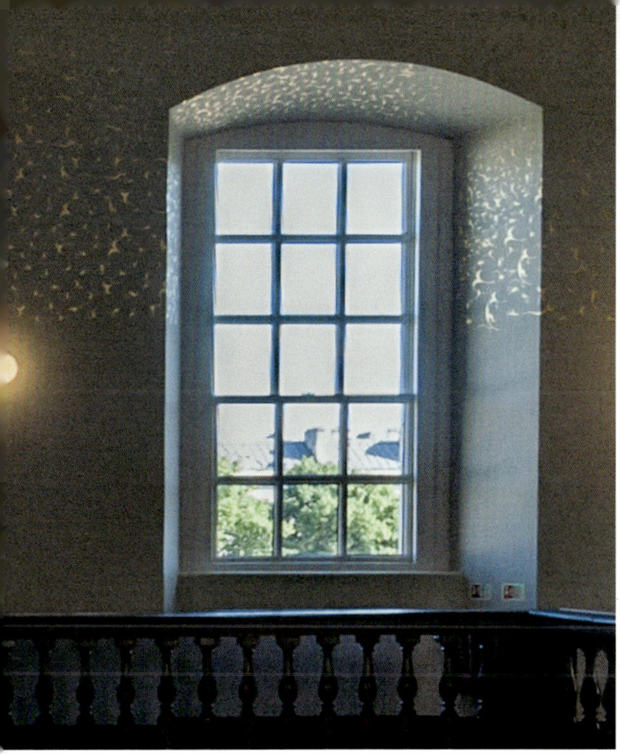

◀ *Richard Wright's artwork as seen from the Great Hall balcony.*

in a Baroque style popular at the courts of Catholic Europe but almost completely alien in 1630s England. Complemented by further large-scale paintings by Orazio on the walls below, antique marble statues and possibly Gian Lorenzo Bernini's famed bust of Charles I, the ceiling of the Great Hall set the tone for the decoration of the rest of the House. As such, the Hall would have announced the Queen's House (to the small elite who had the privilege of entering it) as being at the cutting edge of taste and cultural patronage, though its decoration would also come to demonstrate the Queen's 'Catholic influence' to a Protestant England deeply suspicious of her connections with the Vatican. It is notable, particularly in the context of the female domain of the Queen's House, that all 26 figures in the paintings are women: in a trope all too familiar throughout history, opponents of the monarchy were quick to seize on what was seen as the 'undue' female power wielded by the Queen over her husband.

The ceiling canvases were reserved to the State after Charles's execution, when the House was stripped of artworks, then possibly stored and replaced in 1661 after the Restoration of Charles II in 1660. By 1708 they had been removed for good and Queen Anne put them at the disposal of her favourite, Sarah Churchill, Duchess of Marlborough. The Duchess had them installed a few years later in her new London residence, Marlborough House on Pall Mall (now the headquarters of the Commonwealth). As the ceiling there is smaller than that in the Queen's House, the canvases unfortunately had to be cut down, severely compromising their condition and distorting their perspective.

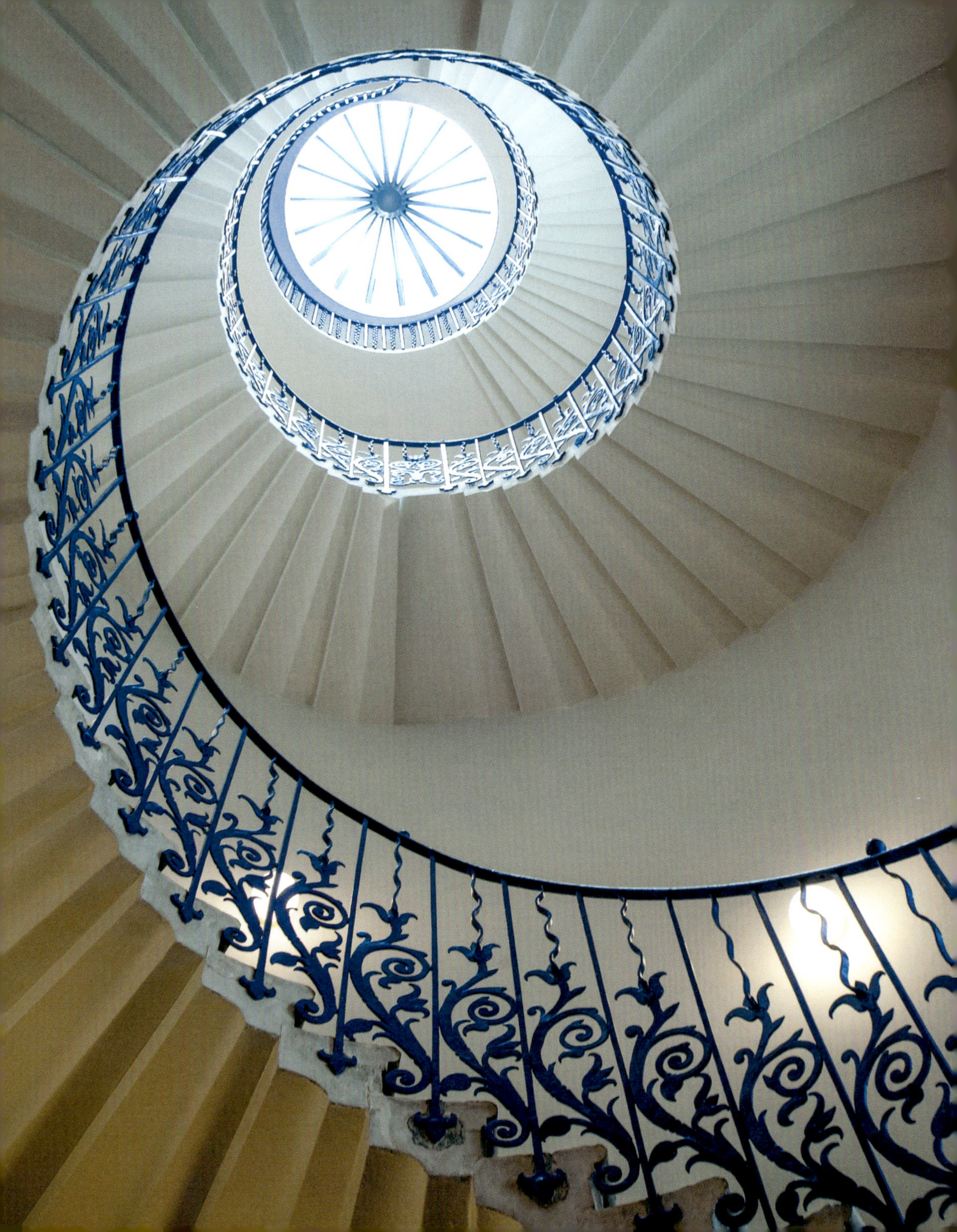

Tulip Stairs

This icon of the Queen's House, the so-called 'Tulip Stairs', is the earliest centrally unsupported spiral stairway in England, based on the Italian Renaissance model. The wrought-iron rail design of what Inigo Jones called the 'round stairs' was first referred to as 'tulips' in an account for a smith's repairs in 1694, but the flowers are more probably lilies, the royal flower of France, in compliment to Henrietta Maria. The stairs have strength as well as elegance: their design is based on compression, with their precisely cut stone treads locking into each other and the enclosing wall.

The position of the stairs, off the south-east corner of the Great Hall, and the lack of resting points below the upper floor, indicate that it was primarily conceived as a descending flight, enabling access to the Hall from the rooms on the first floor above. Those coming across the Central Bridge appear dramatically on the gallery through an imposing doorway with the Royal Arms above, and can also subsequently 'make an entrance' into the Hall by descending the Tulip Stairs. In reverse – that is, ascending the stairs and crossing the Centre Bridge north to south – the route is undramatic until one emerges into view from the park below through the central door of the south loggia. Above first-floor level, however, there are two small landings on the Tulip Stairs at 15-step intervals which aid ascent to a larger one at the top. This originally gave access to the roof for views over the palace and along the river, via a wooden turret that was removed in about 1822. The extension of the staircase into the basement is not original and dates only from the 19th century.

◀ *The Tulip Stairs.*

Queen's Presence Chamber

When the House was first completed for Henrietta Maria, this room was the Queen's Bedchamber. The ceiling border is original to this period and is now thought to be by the decorative painter Edward Pearce senior, who collaborated with Inigo Jones elsewhere. It is in the Italian mannerist style, probably copied via French pattern-books and teeming with grotesques and imaginary architectural features. The corners of the painted surround bear Latin mottos translating as 'Mutual fruitfulness / the hope of the state / burns forever [:]/ beauty [or splendour] with fragrance'. The inscription HENRICA MARIA REGINA appears in the coving over the fire, while opposite, above what would have been the position of the bed, are the royal arms of France and England set together in heart-shaped form.

The original intention had been for this border to frame a vast canvas spanning the centre part of the ceiling and painted by Guido Reni, one of the leading Italian painters of the period, and one of Henrietta Maria's favourite contemporary artists. This was to depict 'Bacchus and Ariadne', the meeting of these two lovers from classical mythology. While the subject was appropriate for a bedchamber, the nudity in which Bacchus and Ariadne were shown did not go without comment from contemporaries who saw the picture. The commission was brokered by the Vatican through Cardinal Francesco Barberini, one of the leading art patrons of Baroque Rome, and though it was completed and much admired in Rome, where it was sent before its intended dispatch to England, the painting never made it to the Queen's House. Henrietta Maria eventually took delivery of it in exile in France, where she was eventually forced to sell it for financial reasons. It was subsequently cut-up by the widow of the purchaser, reputedly owing to its 'improper' nudity, but more probably due to its sheer size and the fact that pictorially coherent smaller fragments were more saleable than the whole.

In about 1640 Henrietta Maria had another picture, already in the Royal Collection, installed where the Reni had been supposed to go: Giulio Romano's *Daedalus and Icarus*. Romano's painting was ranked behind only the Gentileschi ceiling paintings as the most valuable art work in the House in the 1649 inventory drawn up for the public sale of 'the Late King's Goods' following Charles I's execution. Although reserved from the sale, it disappeared at some point during the Commonwealth. How the gap was filled is unclear until the present canvas of 'Aurora dispersing the shades

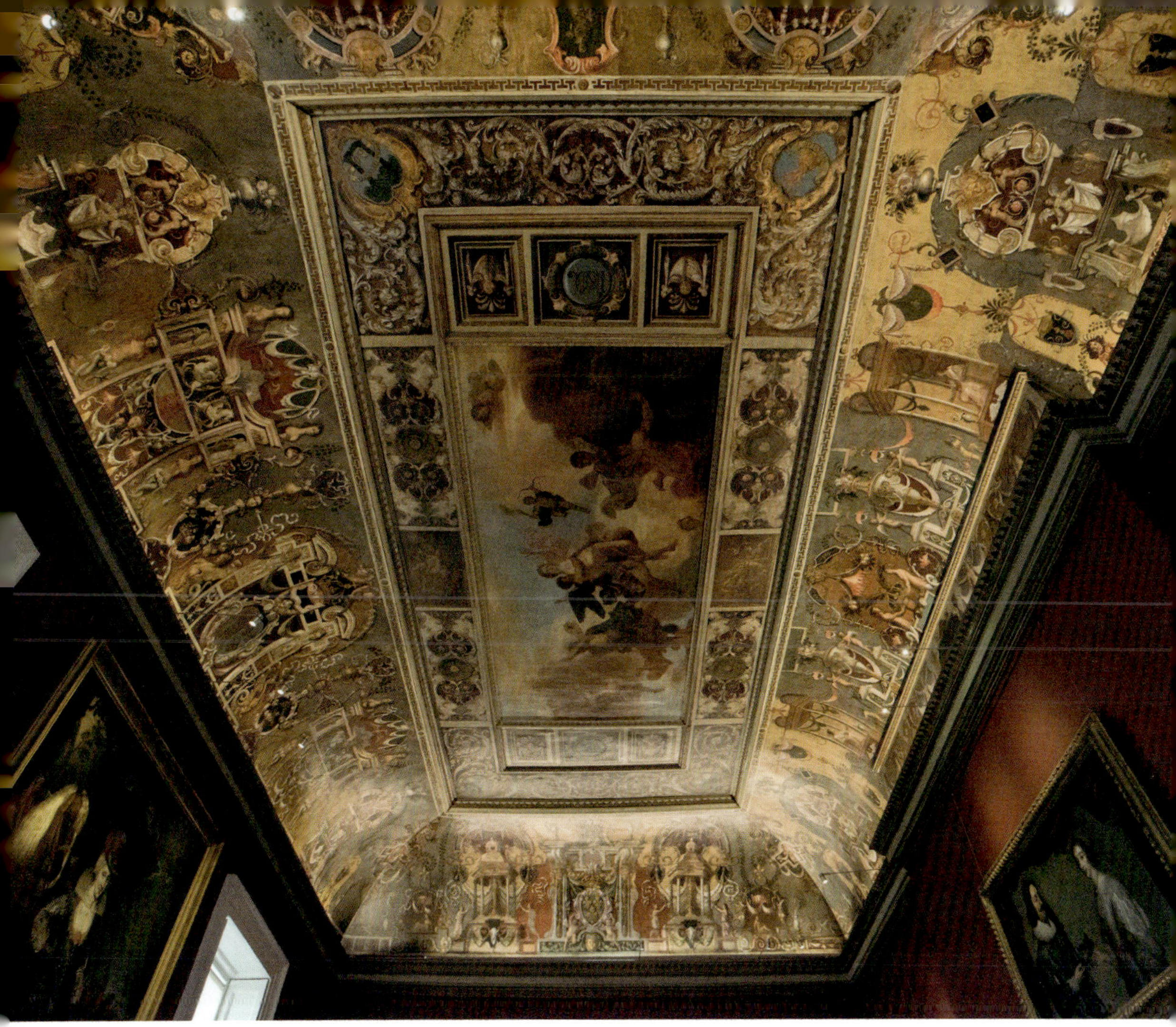

▲ *A section of the ceiling of the Queen's Presence Chamber.*

of Night' arrived. When and how this was acquired is uncertain, as is the identity of the artist and even whether it was painted in the late 17th or early 18th century.

Following the Restoration and the reorganisation of the House into notional king's and queen's sides, thanks to addition of the East and West Bridge Rooms, this room became the Queen's Presence Chamber.

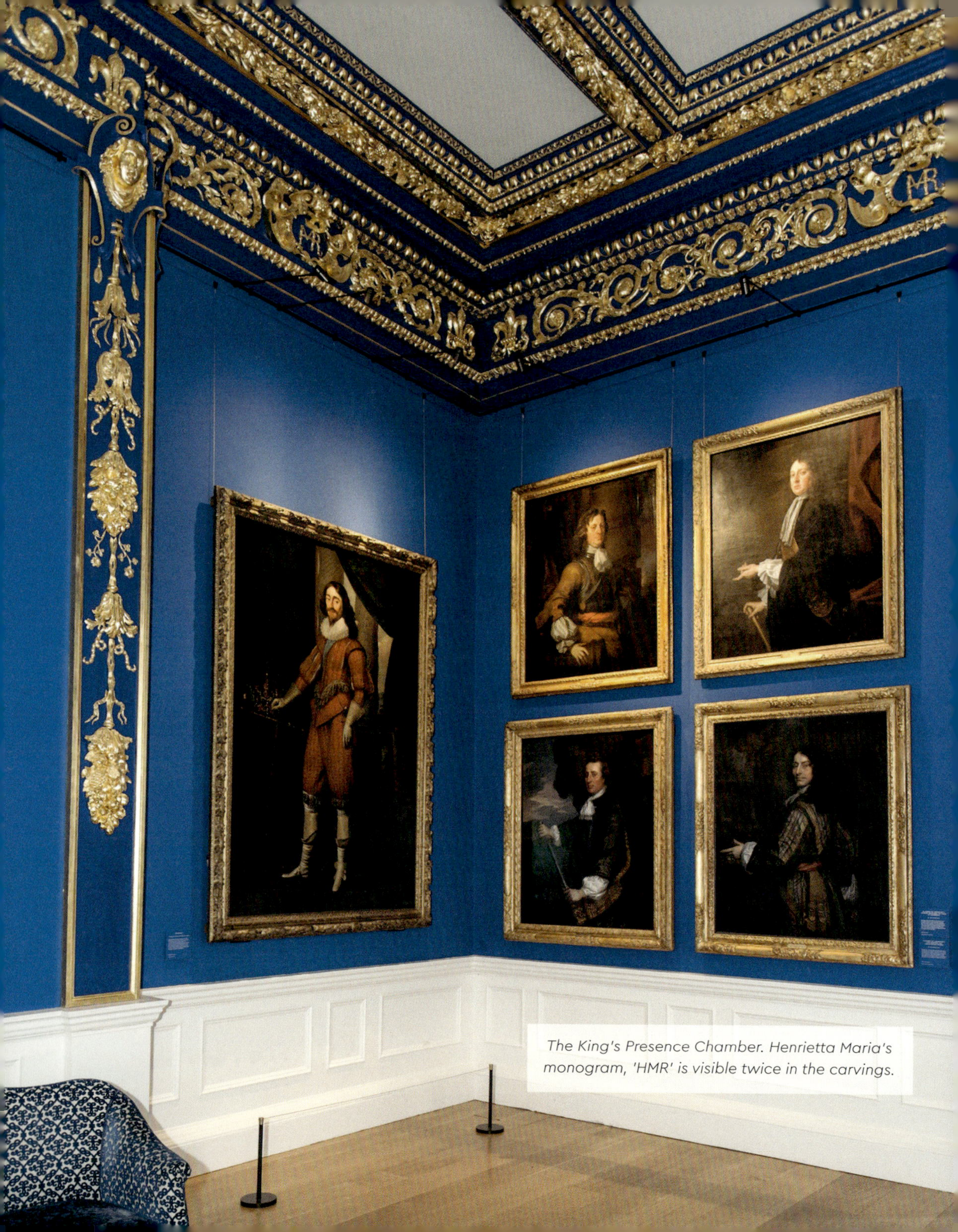

The King's Presence Chamber. Henrietta Maria's monogram, 'HMR' is visible twice in the carvings.

King's Presence Chamber

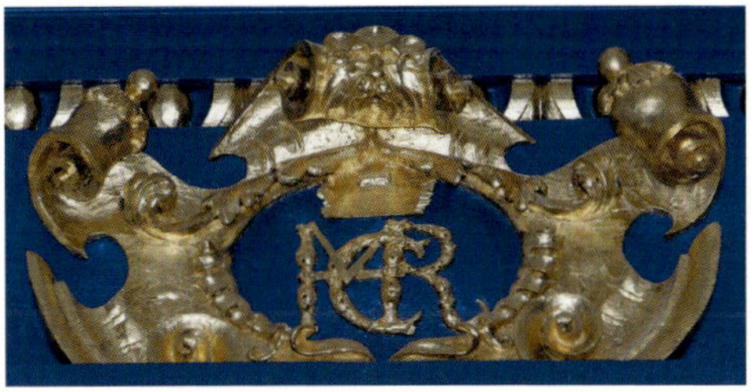

▲ *A monogram seen in the room's detailing.*

This room would have been the most richly decorated space in the House during Henrietta Maria's initial occupation, when it was designated as the 'Queen's Withdrawing Chamber'. The present colour scheme of gilded blue reflects what seems to have been the original one of the elaborate carved woodwork. Its splendid detailing takes in festoons of fruit and flowers, masks and fleur-de-lys (this emblem of the Bourbon monarchy, referring to Henrietta Maria's French origins) as well as the intertwined CR/HM (Carolus Rex [King Charles]/Henrietta Maria) and HMR (Henrietta Maria Regina) monograms. A series of 22 canvases by the Flemish painter Jacob Jordaens representing the story of Cupid and Psyche were commissioned for the walls and ceiling. These arrived progressively, and some ultimately not at all, but in the interim other works from the Royal Collection were displayed. They included Orazio Gentileschi's *Lot and his Daughters* (later moved to the Hall), Artemisia Gentileschi's *Tarquin and Lucretia* and Tintoretto's *The Muses* as well as works by Van Dyck and Giulio Romano, among others.

From 1662, when the house was remodelled under Charles II and the east side of the House became the 'King's Side', this room became the King's Presence Chamber, though it was never used as such.

Central Bridge Room

This room was originally the only bridge between the north and south sides of the House in Inigo Jones's design for an H-shaped building spanning the walled public road between Woolwich and Deptford. Under the orientation of the House originally envisaged for Anne of Denmark, in which the primary façade was that facing south towards the park, it would have formed part of the ceremonial route from the park over into the gallery of the Great Hall. Whether the Royal Arms over the door opening from the bridge were part of Jones's 1616 intentions is unknown. The fact that they were placed there under Henrietta Maria, however, shows that the idea of such a south-to-north route was still then in mind.

The view from the windows on either side of the room would have originally been east and west along the road. Following the remodelling of the House under Charles II, this long view was blocked by the East and West Bridge Rooms. These later bridge insertions retain their fine moulded ceilings by Charles II's Master Plasterer, John Grove, and originally had balconies over the public road (see page 42). Perhaps on account of the rather uninviting nature of the muddy road – or the opportunity for insult from it – these balconies were short-lived features.

South Stairs and Orangery

The Orangery has long been called such, but only because of its form and Henrietta Maria's known interest in such cultivation: it was never used as a space for growing exotic plants and fruit. Jones undoubtedly designed the Orangery as a transitional space: a vestibule for entry from or exit to the park, consistent with the House's use as a hunting lodge. Its inner wall has the same exterior-form windows as those originally in the House's ground-floor outer walls. It also once had a 12-foot-high pair of central 'air-lock' doors, of which only hinge pintles remain, opening inwards to the central south corridor. It is easy to imagine riders arriving from the park, dismounting outside the open exterior door and entering for refreshments, or leaving their horses with grooms and using the House in its bridge function to cross privately to the palace side.

If, as has been suggested, the House was originally conceived under Anne of Denmark as a new visual frontispiece and route for privileged entry to the palace from the park, the elegant South Stairs were designed as 'ascending' stairs. Their two landings, suitable resting points for those going up in heavy garments or gowns, suggest this, in contrast to the (probably 'descending') Tulip Stairs on the north side of the house,

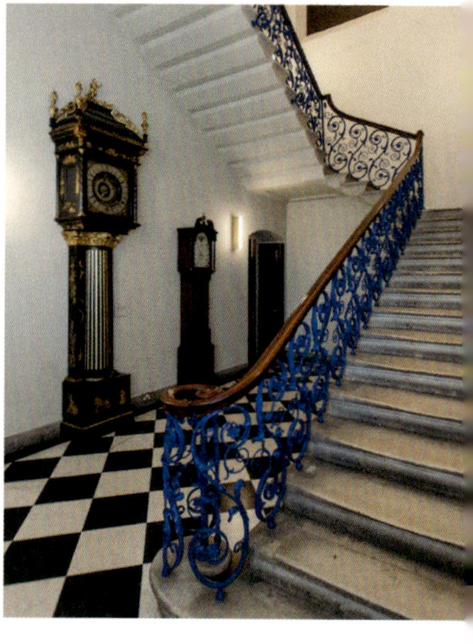

▶ *The South Stairs.*

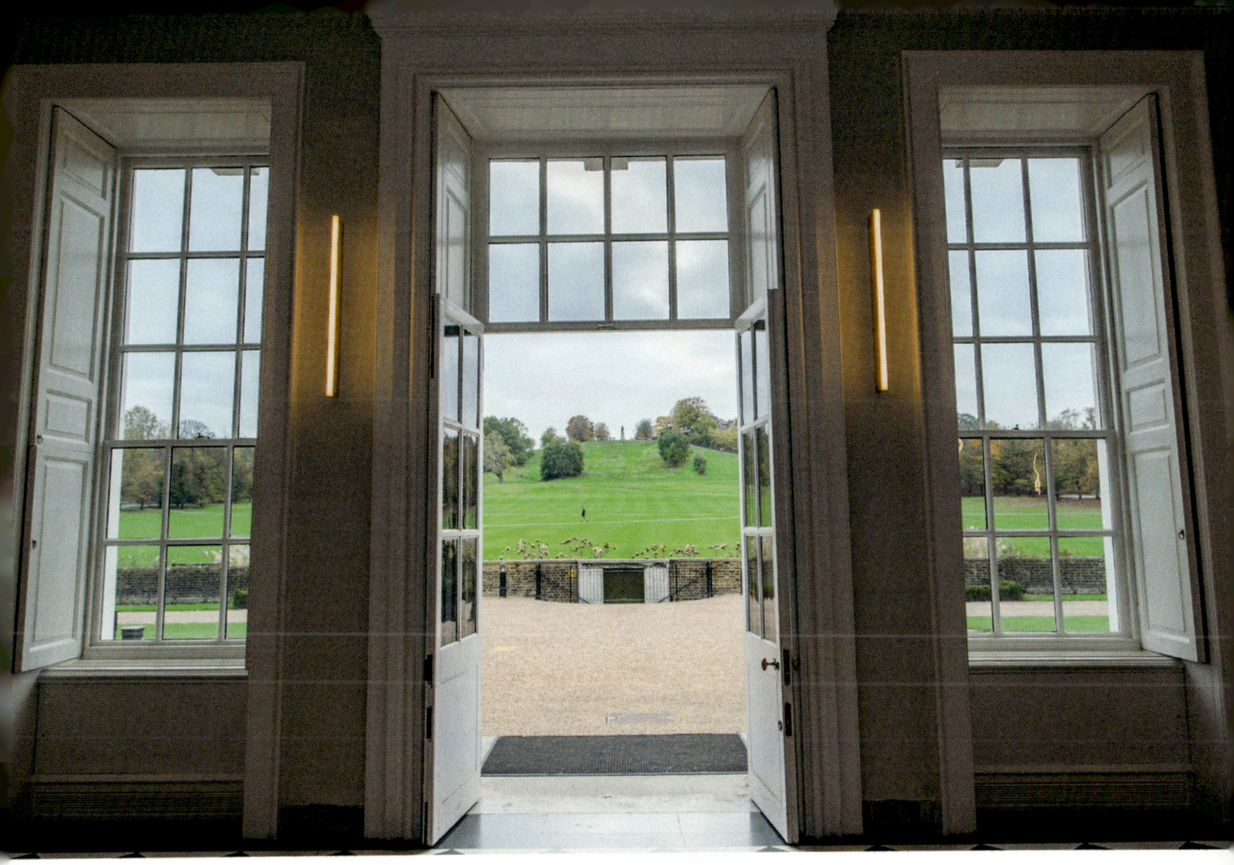

▲ *The Orangery.*

which has no such landings between the Hall and first-floor level. Jones's original balustrade design is unknown and, by the 1930s, there was just a utilitarian early 19th-century railing in place: the present rococo balustrade was installed in 1936 from Pembroke House, Whitehall (1724), when this was demolished to build the new Ministry of Defence.

During Henrietta Maria's brief residence in 1662–3 as Queen Dowager, the South Stairs, on what was by then the 'Queen's (west) Side' of the House, would have served as a 'back' entrance to her private apartments, leading as they do almost straight to her Bedchamber (the room occupying the south-west corner of the first floor). This would have been a convenient arrangement for Henrietta Maria's purposes, particularly since the Bedchamber had been partitioned to create a small cabinet adjacent that probably functioned as a private chapel. The South Stairs would have provided direct and discreet access for a Catholic priest to minister to the Queen's private devotions.

An essential introduction to the art collection at the Queen's House.

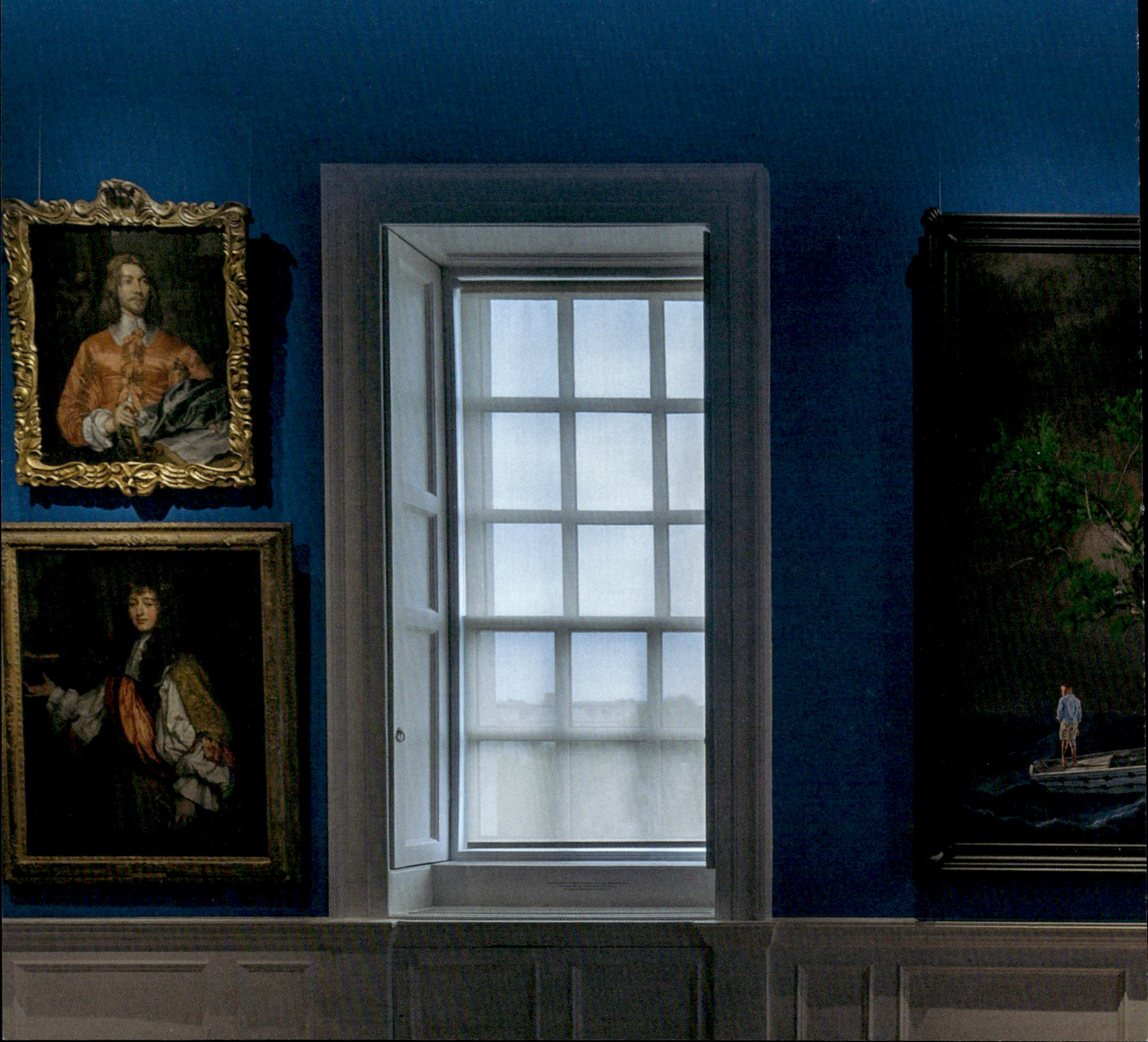

The Queen's House in 20 objects

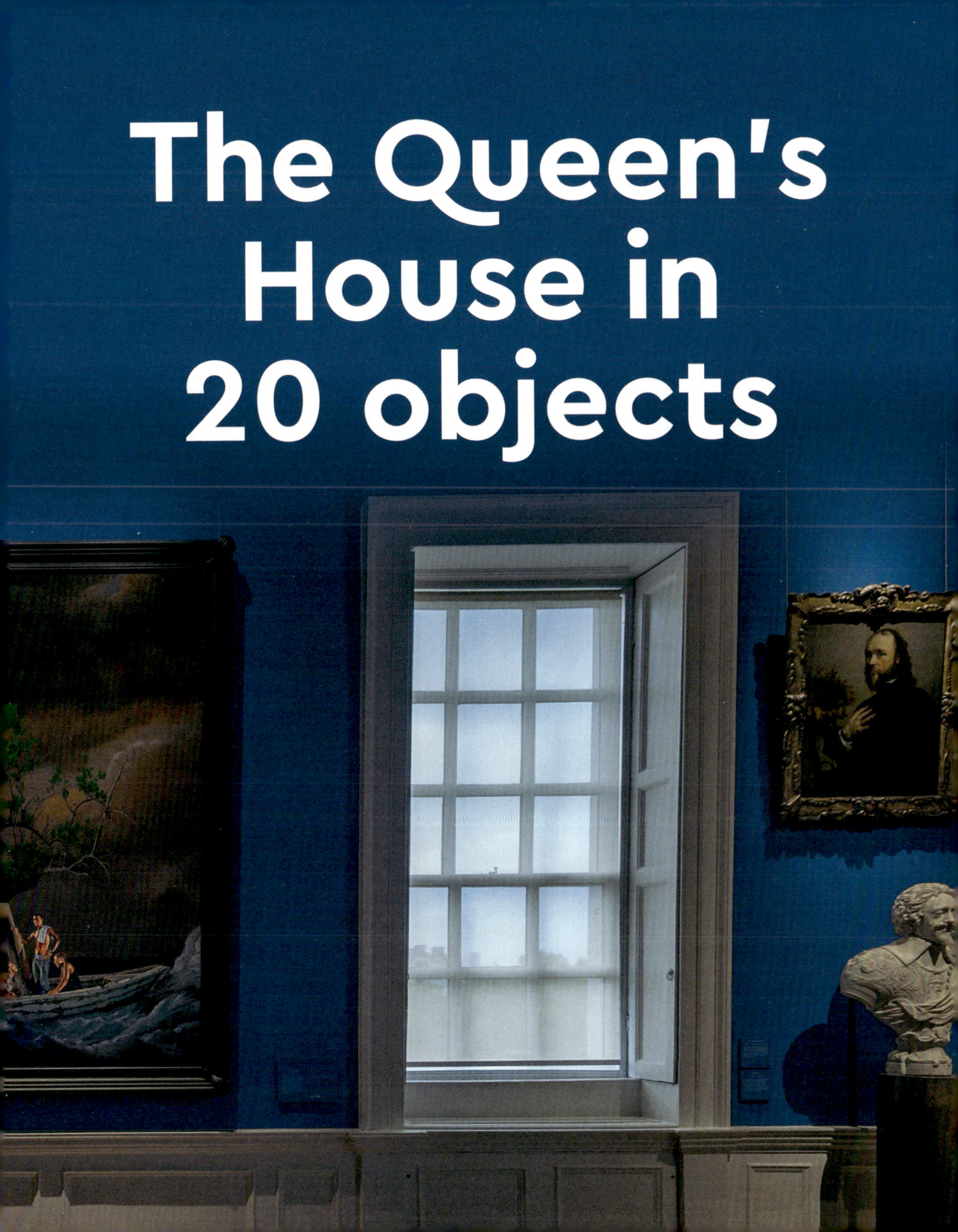

Elizabeth I, the Armada Portrait, *16th-century English school, about 1588.*
The iconic 'Armada Portrait' of Elizabeth I was painted to commemorate the successful repelling of the Spanish Armada in 1588. Elizabeth turns her back on a gloomy painting of wrecked Spanish ships, a counterpoint to a sunnier, more serene image of the English fleet preparing to engage the enemy. Presenting Elizabeth as a pillar of strength, the painting obscures both the vulnerability of England and Elizabeth herself in the face of the Armada, and the extent to which the outcome of what was in fact a delicately balanced conflict was determined by the weather.

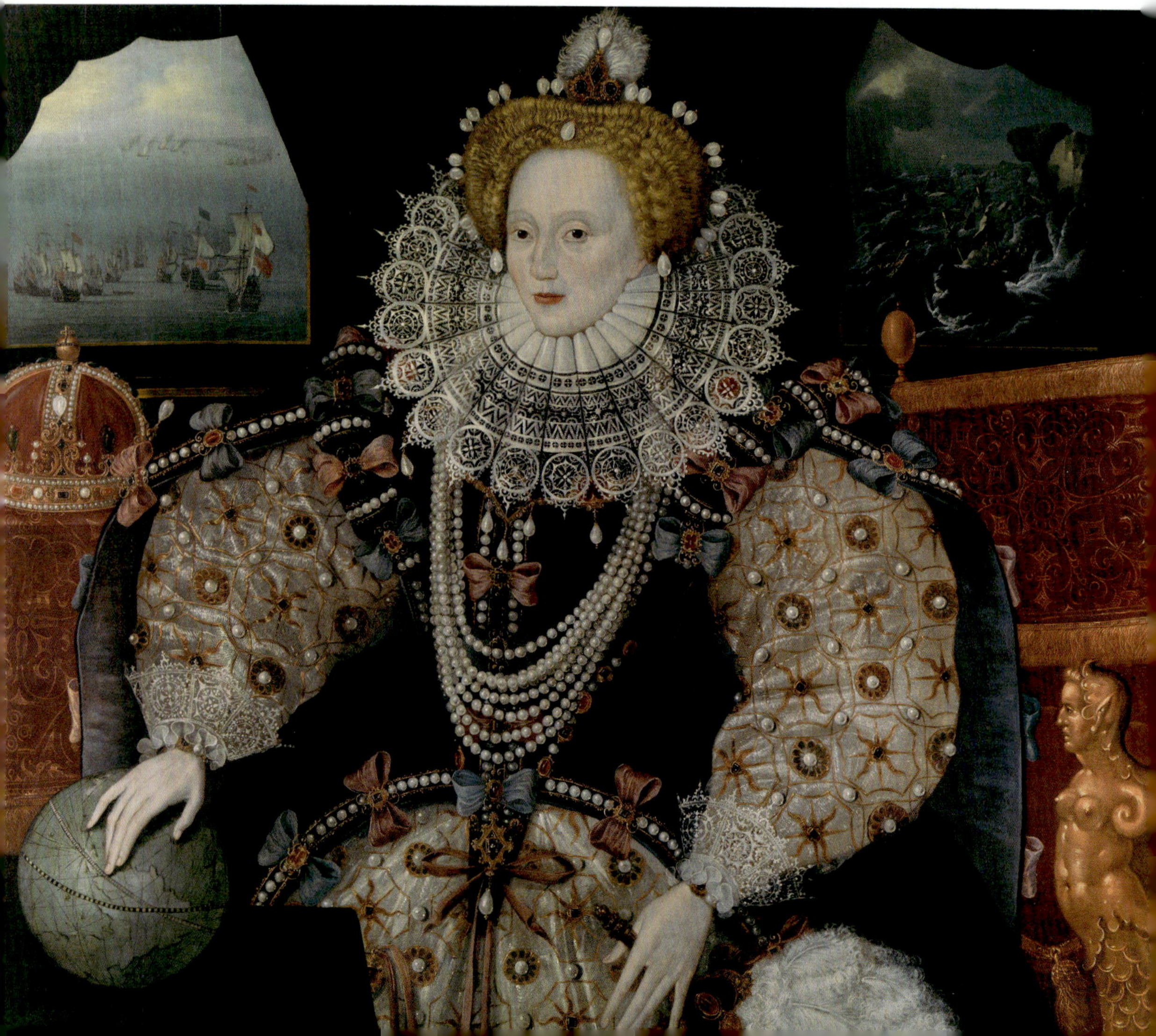

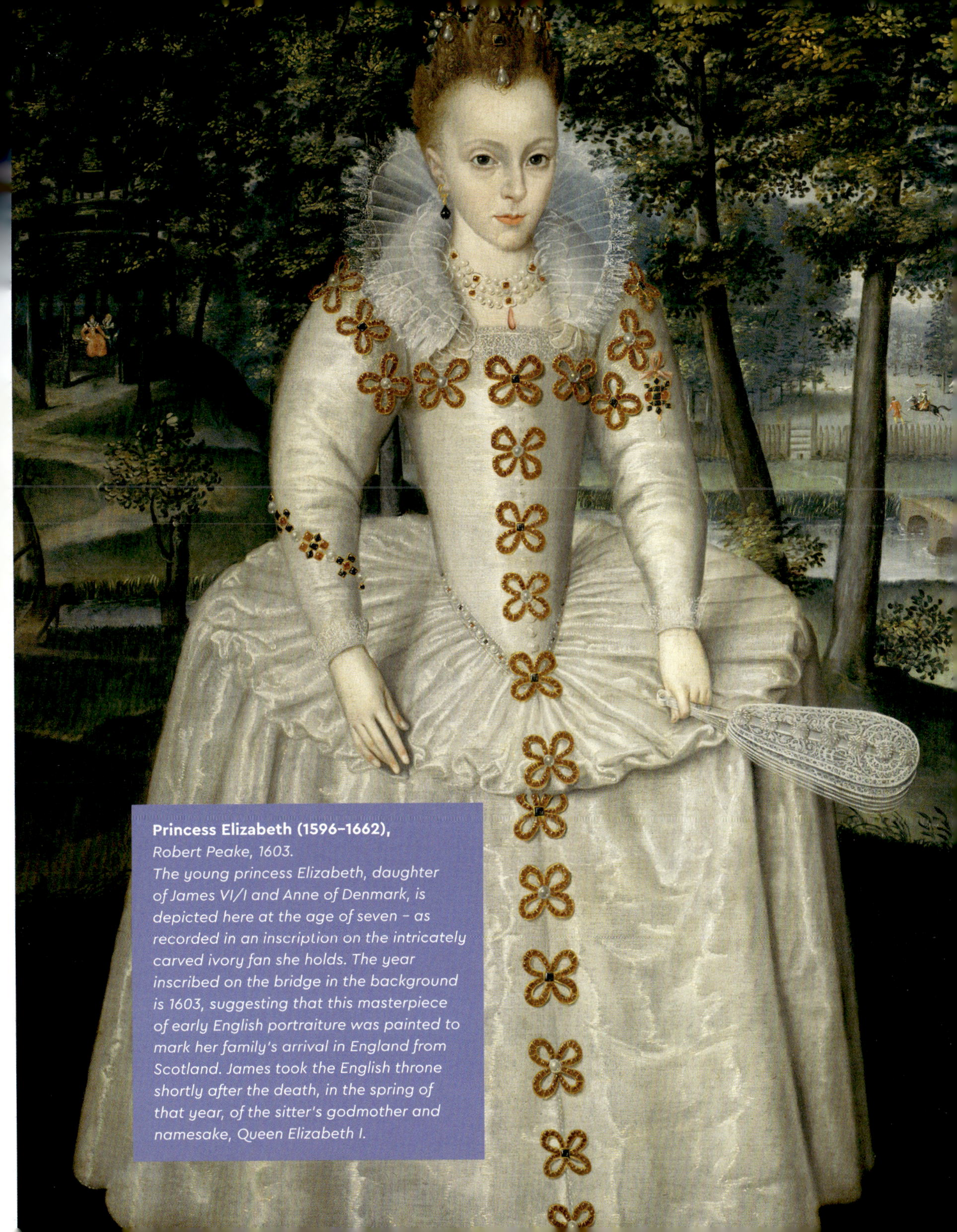

Princess Elizabeth (1596–1662),
Robert Peake, 1603.
The young princess Elizabeth, daughter of James VI/I and Anne of Denmark, is depicted here at the age of seven – as recorded in an inscription on the intricately carved ivory fan she holds. The year inscribed on the bridge in the background is 1603, suggesting that this masterpiece of early English portraiture was painted to mark her family's arrival in England from Scotland. James took the English throne shortly after the death, in the spring of that year, of the sitter's godmother and namesake, Queen Elizabeth I.

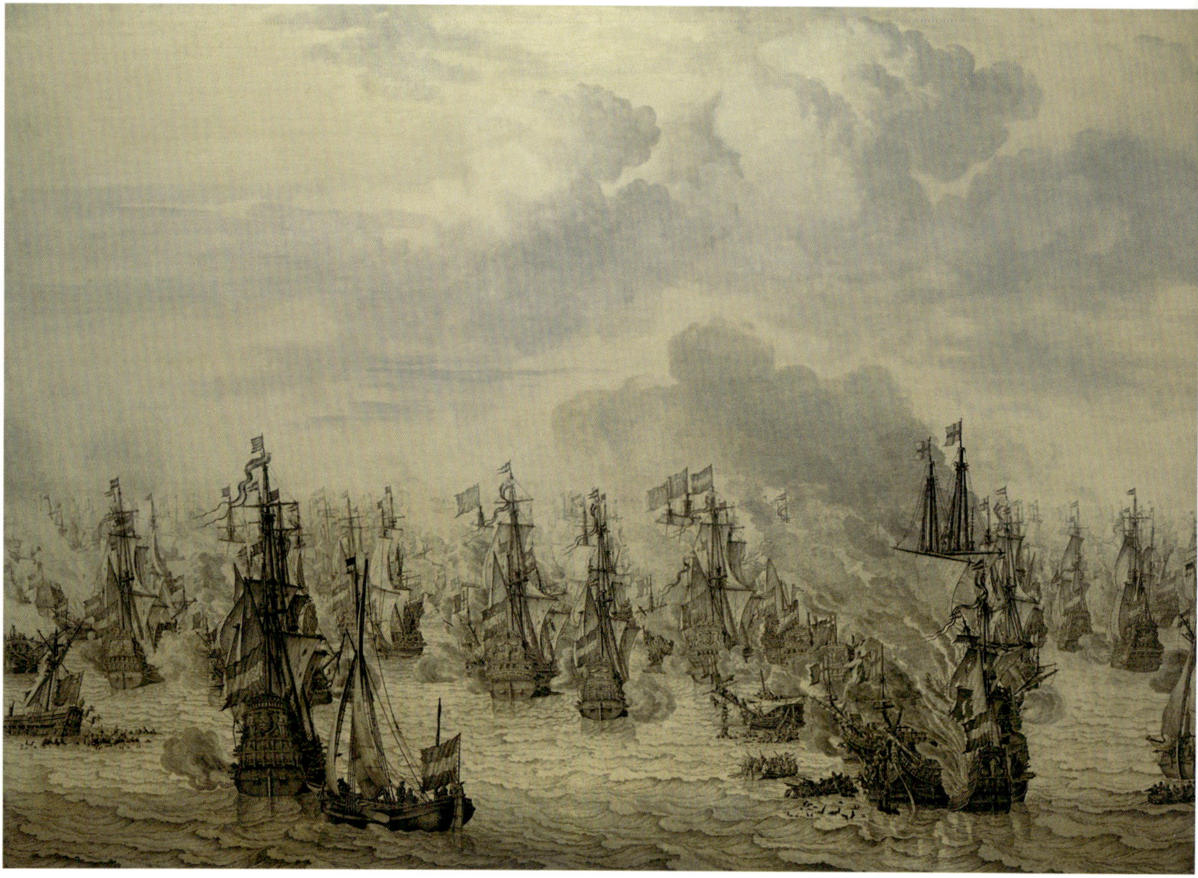

The Battle of Scheveningen, *Willem van de Velde the Elder, 1655.*
Willem van de Velde the Elder was sought after throughout Europe for his monochrome pictures of marine subjects. Known now as 'pen paintings', they are in fact highly intricate ink drawings on canvas or panel supports which were then varnished. Here Van de Velde depicts the Battle of Scheveningen, a sea battle between the Dutch and the English in 1653. He often sailed out with the Dutch fleet to record it in action for the Admiralty. In the foreground of this picture, wearing a hat and with pen and paper in hand, he has shown himself doing just that.

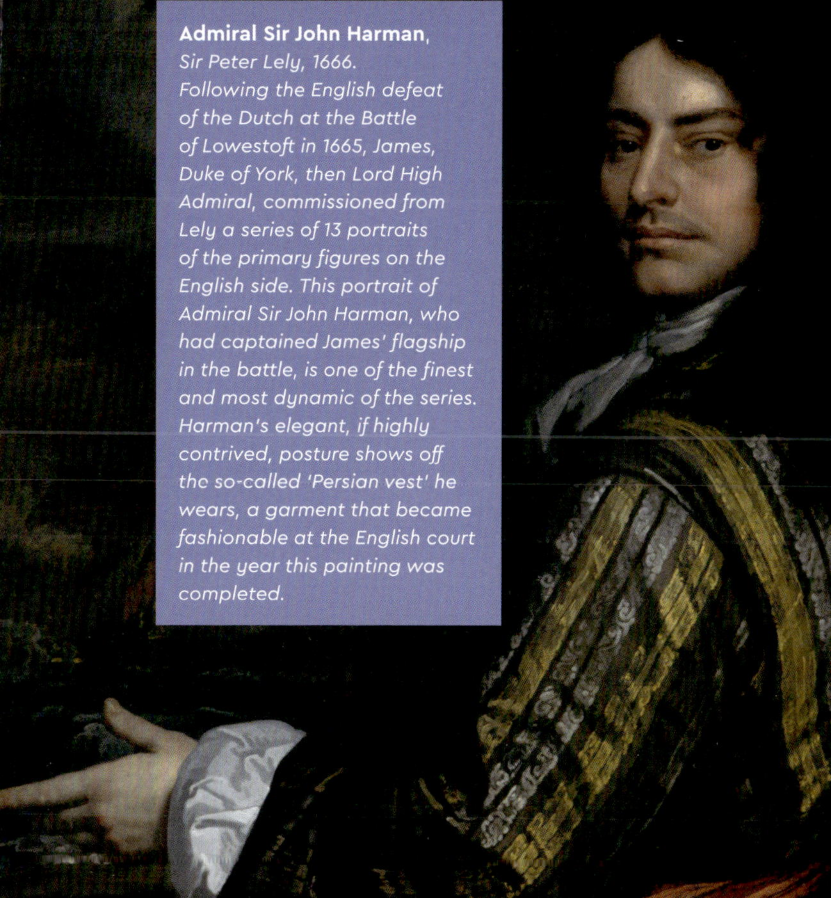

Admiral Sir John Harman, *Sir Peter Lely, 1666.* *Following the English defeat of the Dutch at the Battle of Lowestoft in 1665, James, Duke of York, then Lord High Admiral, commissioned from Lely a series of 13 portraits of the primary figures on the English side. This portrait of Admiral Sir John Harman, who had captained James' flagship in the battle, is one of the finest and most dynamic of the series. Harman's elegant, if highly contrived, posture shows off the so-called 'Persian vest' he wears, a garment that became fashionable at the English court in the year this painting was completed.*

'St Michael' (1669), *unknown, about 1672.*
This is one of the most important ship models, not only in the collection but in the world, being the earliest such model that can be identified as representing a specific ship. This extraordinary object has a rightful place in the Queen's House, both for its superb craftsmanship and for the fact that its identification as the St Michael *is verified. This is in part through comparison with intricate drawings of the full-sized vessel, no doubt taken from first-hand observation by the artists Willem van de Velde father and son who had their studio in the Queen's House.*

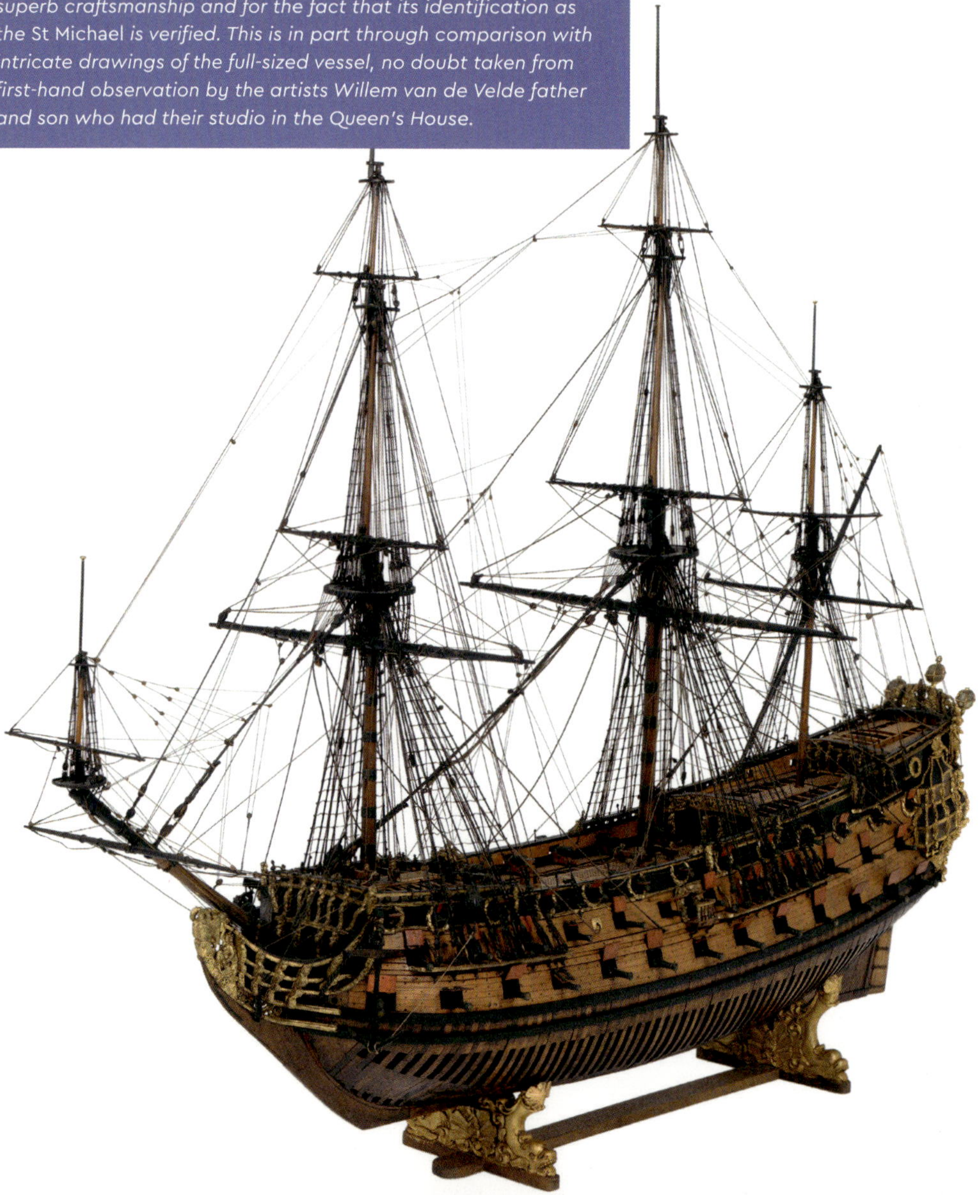

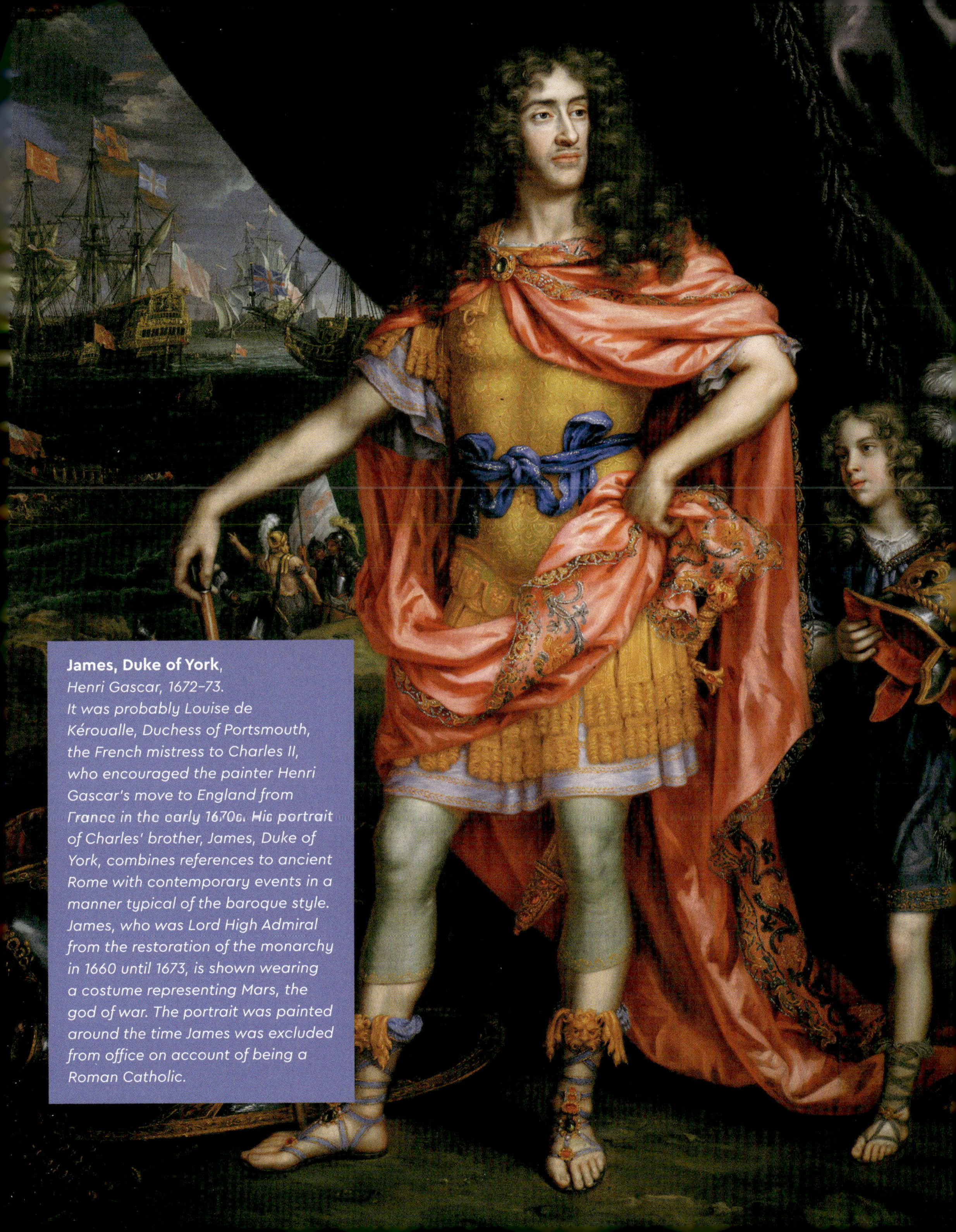

James, Duke of York,
Henri Gascar, 1672–73.
It was probably Louise de Kéroualle, Duchess of Portsmouth, the French mistress to Charles II, who encouraged the painter Henri Gascar's move to England from France in the early 1670s. His portrait of Charles' brother, James, Duke of York, combines references to ancient Rome with contemporary events in a manner typical of the baroque style. James, who was Lord High Admiral from the restoration of the monarchy in 1660 until 1673, is shown wearing a costume representing Mars, the god of war. The portrait was painted around the time James was excluded from office on account of being a Roman Catholic.

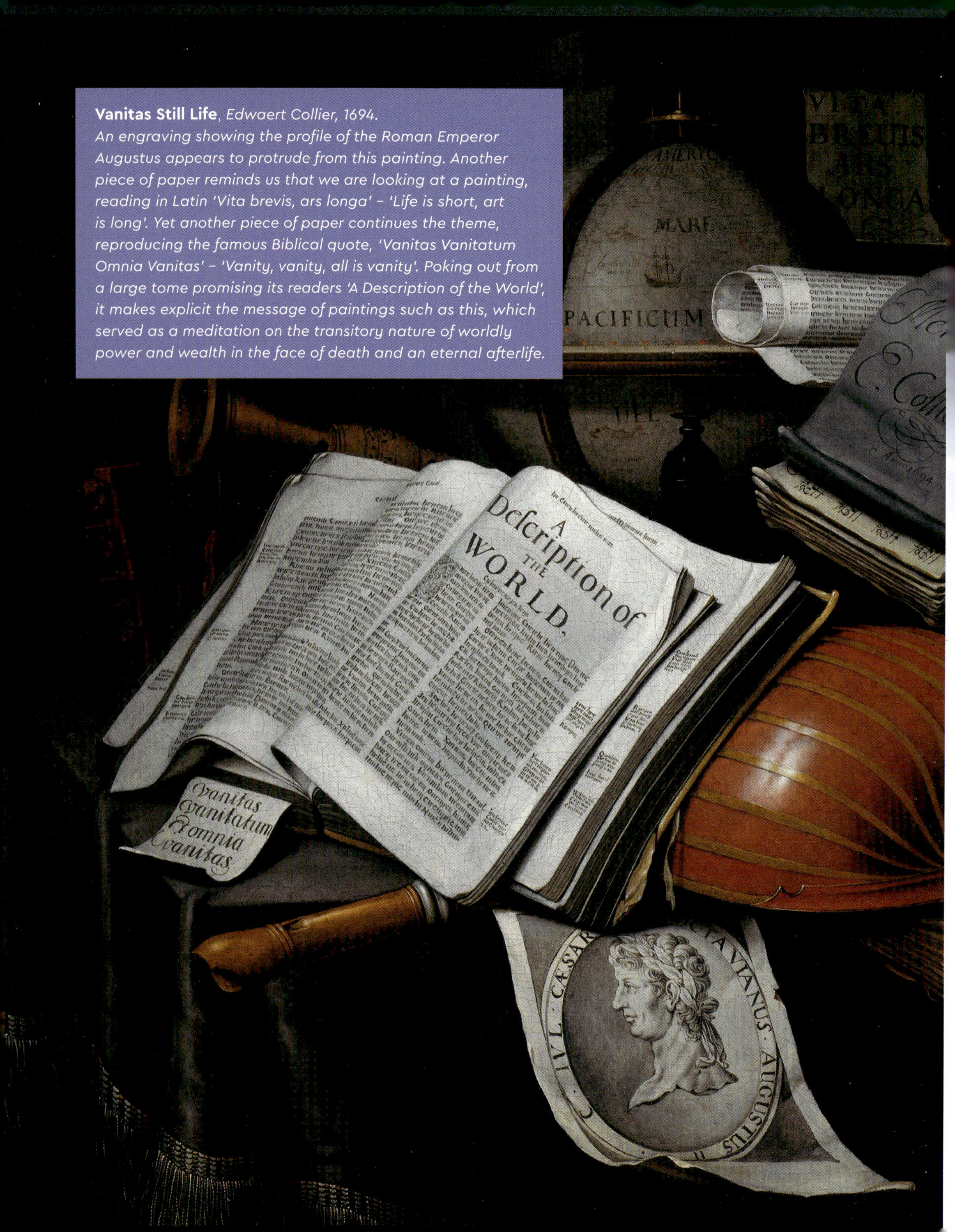

Vanitas Still Life, *Edwaert Collier, 1694.*
An engraving showing the profile of the Roman Emperor Augustus appears to protrude from this painting. Another piece of paper reminds us that we are looking at a painting, reading in Latin 'Vita brevis, ars longa' – 'Life is short, art is long'. Yet another piece of paper continues the theme, reproducing the famous Biblical quote, 'Vanitas Vanitatum Omnia Vanitas' – 'Vanity, vanity, all is vanity'. Poking out from a large tome promising its readers 'A Description of the World', it makes explicit the message of paintings such as this, which served as a meditation on the transitory nature of worldly power and wealth in the face of death and an eternal afterlife.

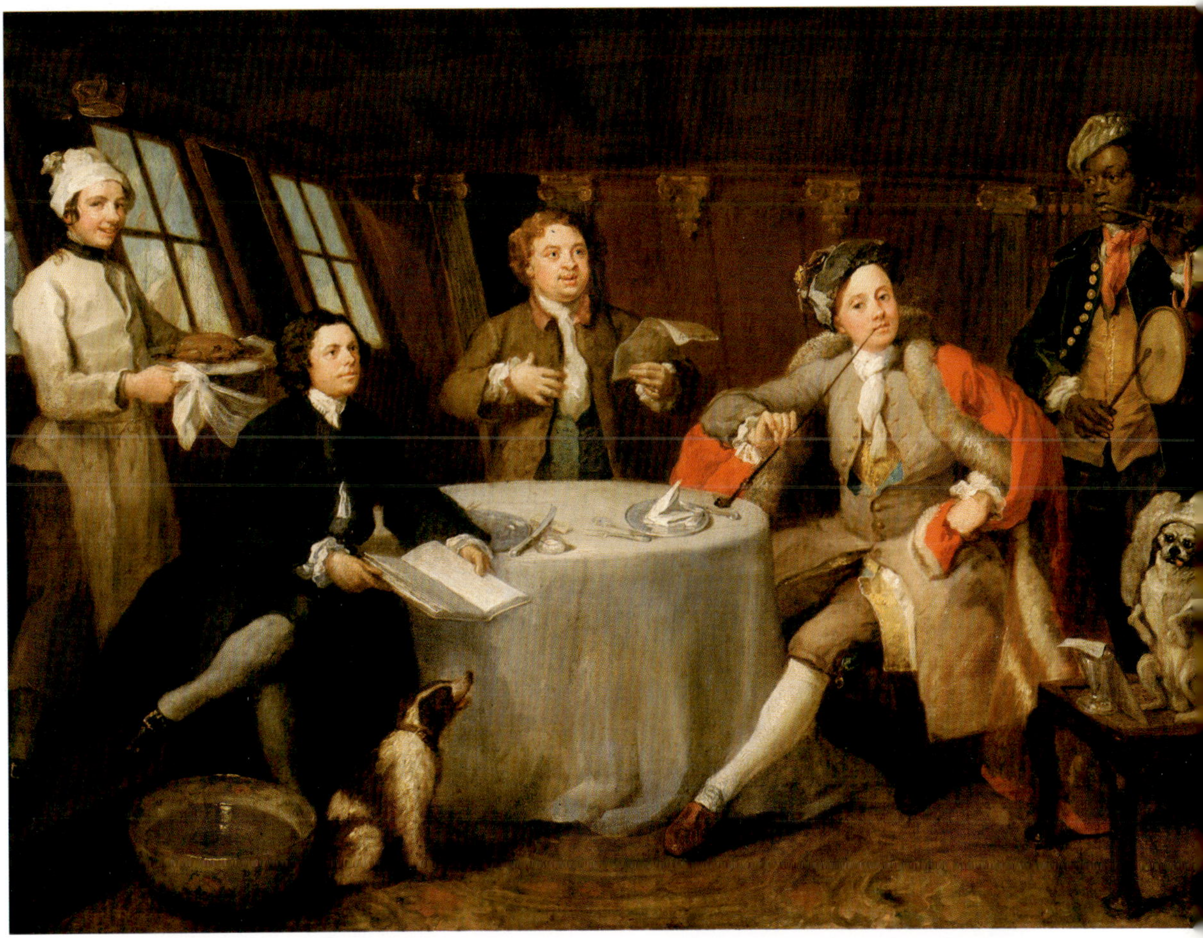

Captain Lord George Graham, in his Cabin, *William Hogarth, 1742–44.*
The master of social observation turns his gaze to the inside of a ship's cabin and the boisterous company of its Captain, Lord George Graham. Like many of Hogarth's scenes, the painting invites us to imagine the cacophony of sounds it encompasses: the voice of the man singing 'Arragh, my Judy', accompanied by the young man playing a pipe and tabor; the yapping of the dogs; the clink of the dinner service and the jangle of the hanging crown compass; and the heavy creaking of the ship's timbers. The pug wearing Captain Graham's wig is Hogarth's own dog, Trump.

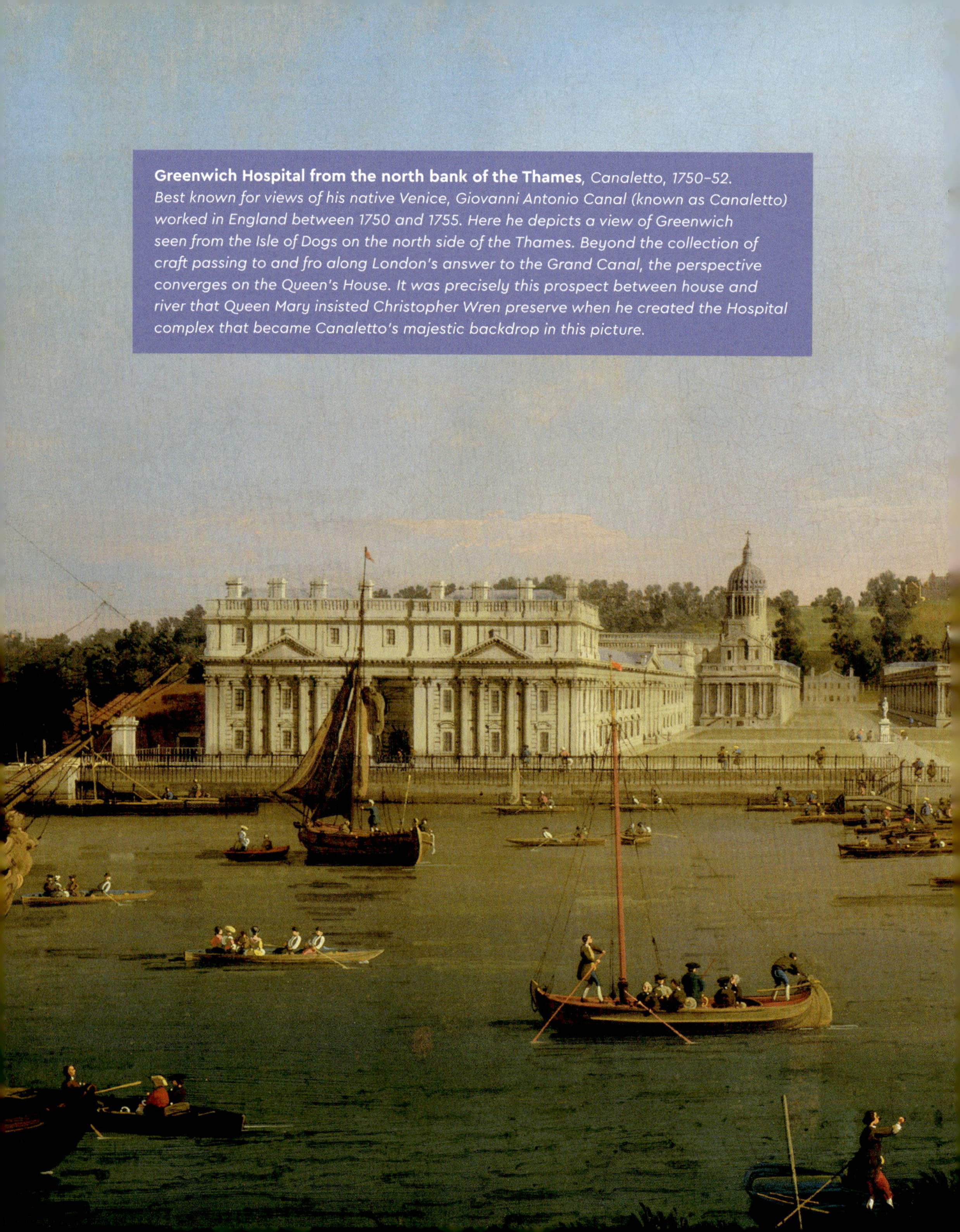

Greenwich Hospital from the north bank of the Thames, *Canaletto, 1750–52.*
Best known for views of his native Venice, Giovanni Antonio Canal (known as Canaletto) worked in England between 1750 and 1755. Here he depicts a view of Greenwich seen from the Isle of Dogs on the north side of the Thames. Beyond the collection of craft passing to and fro along London's answer to the Grand Canal, the perspective converges on the Queen's House. It was precisely this prospect between house and river that Queen Mary insisted Christopher Wren preserve when he created the Hospital complex that became Canaletto's majestic backdrop in this picture.

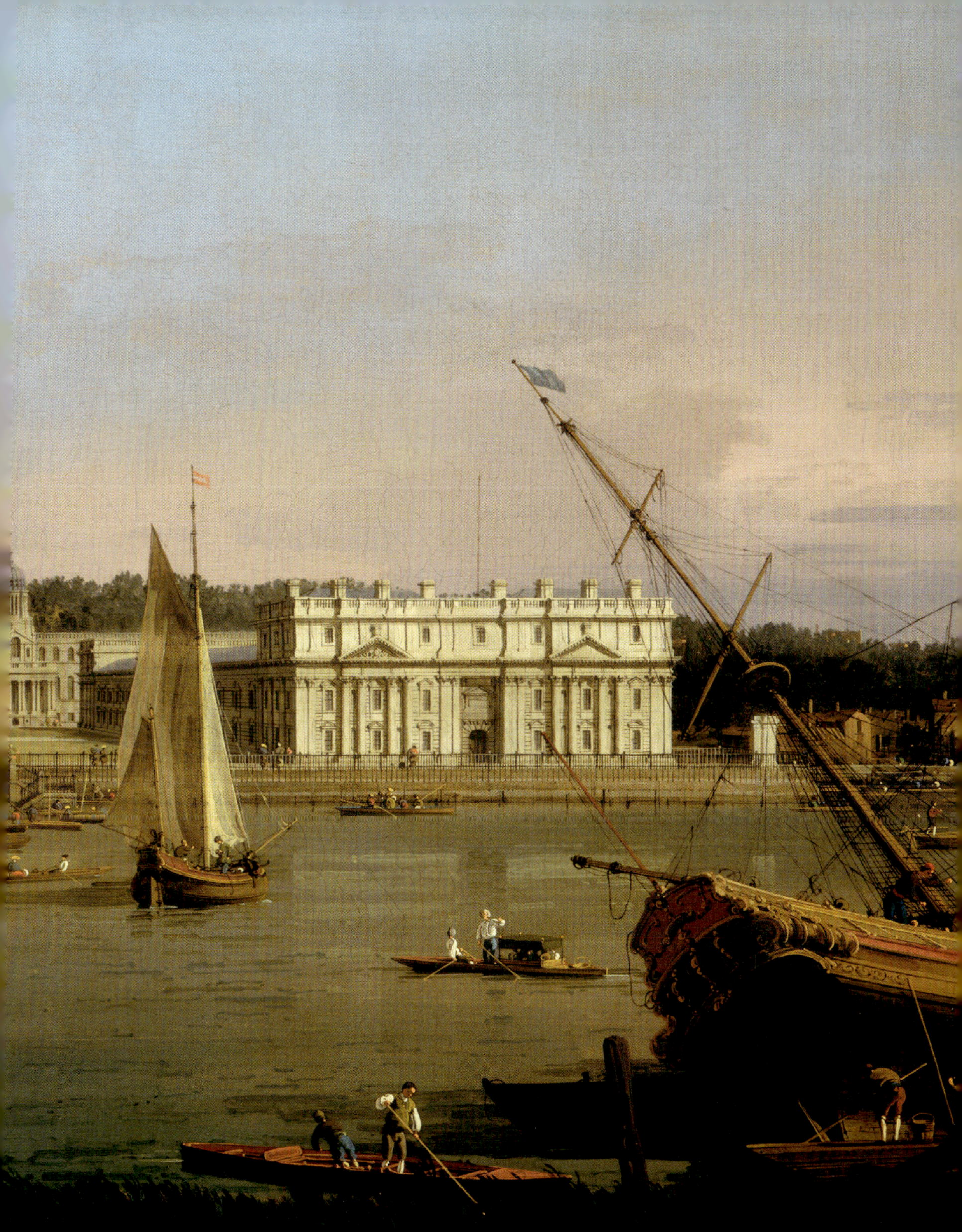

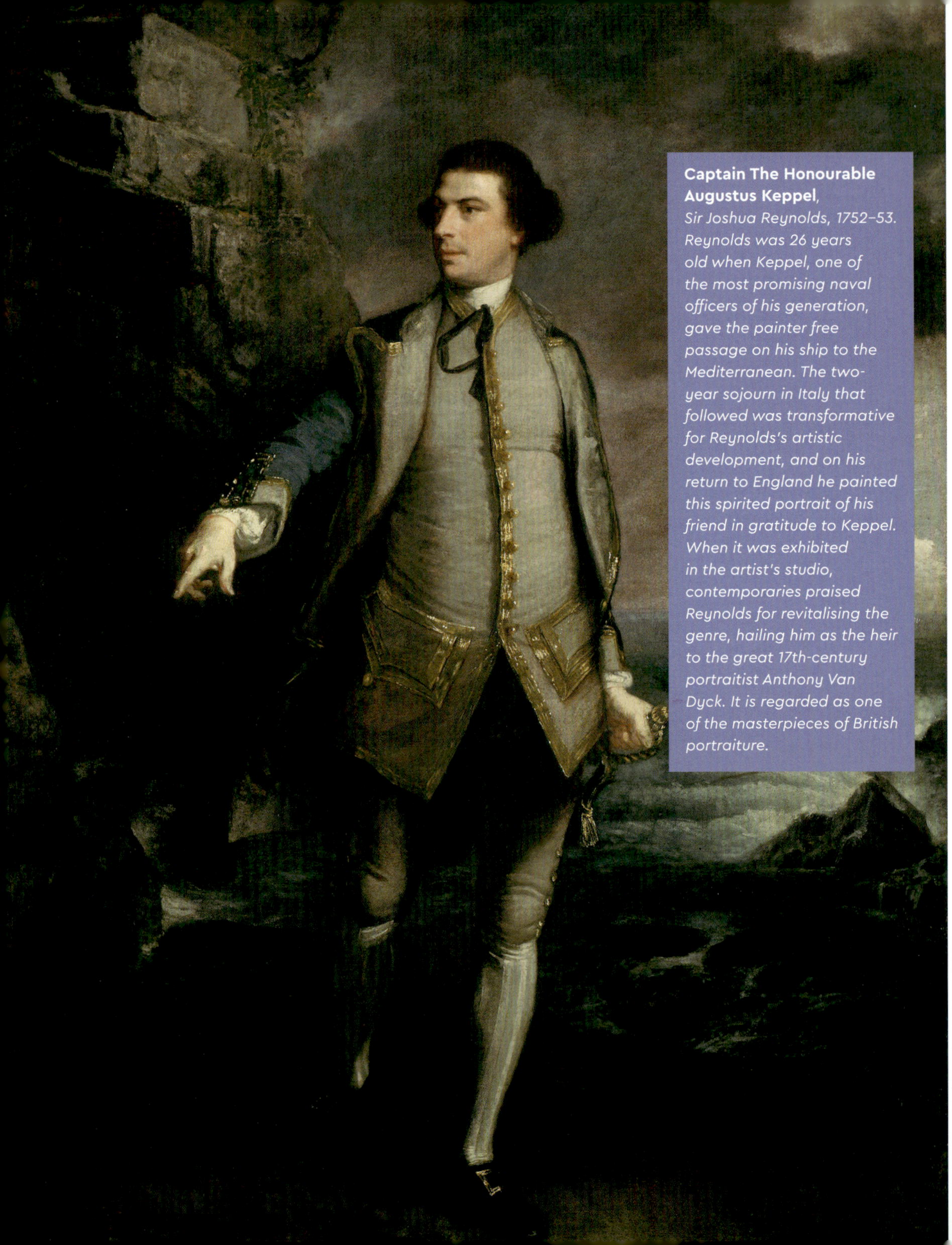

Captain The Honourable Augustus Keppel, *Sir Joshua Reynolds, 1752–53. Reynolds was 26 years old when Keppel, one of the most promising naval officers of his generation, gave the painter free passage on his ship to the Mediterranean. The two-year sojourn in Italy that followed was transformative for Reynolds's artistic development, and on his return to England he painted this spirited portrait of his friend in gratitude to Keppel. When it was exhibited in the artist's studio, contemporaries praised Reynolds for revitalising the genre, hailing him as the heir to the great 17th-century portraitist Anthony Van Dyck. It is regarded as one of the masterpieces of British portraiture.*

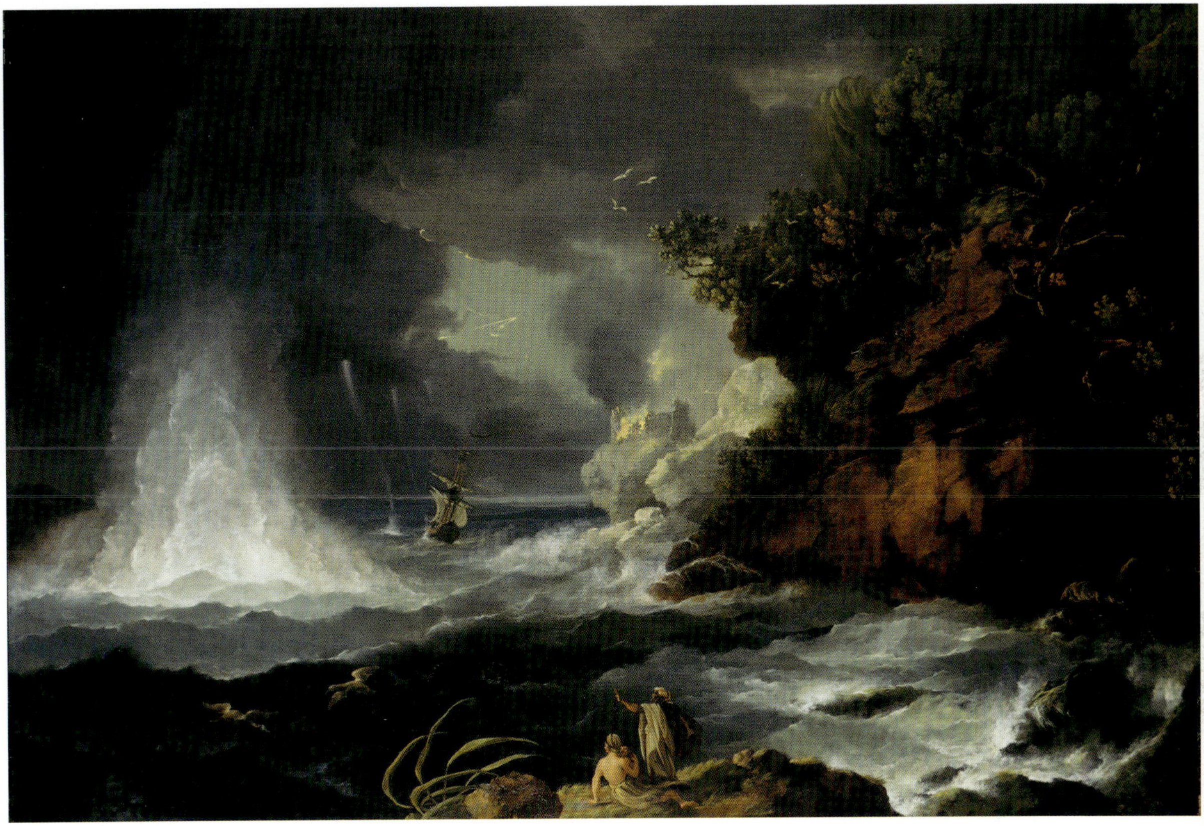

A View of Cape Stephens in Cook's Straits with Waterspout, *William Hodges, 1776. The 27-year-old Hodges embarked on James Cook's second voyage to the Pacific in 1772, and spent the next three years recording in oil sketches and drawings the myriad encounters of the European explorers with the Pacific landscapes and peoples. This dramatic, large-scale painting, which Hodges created in the studio on his return to England, synthesises his memory of multiple real events to produce an image that promotes an idea of the voyage as a classical epic.*

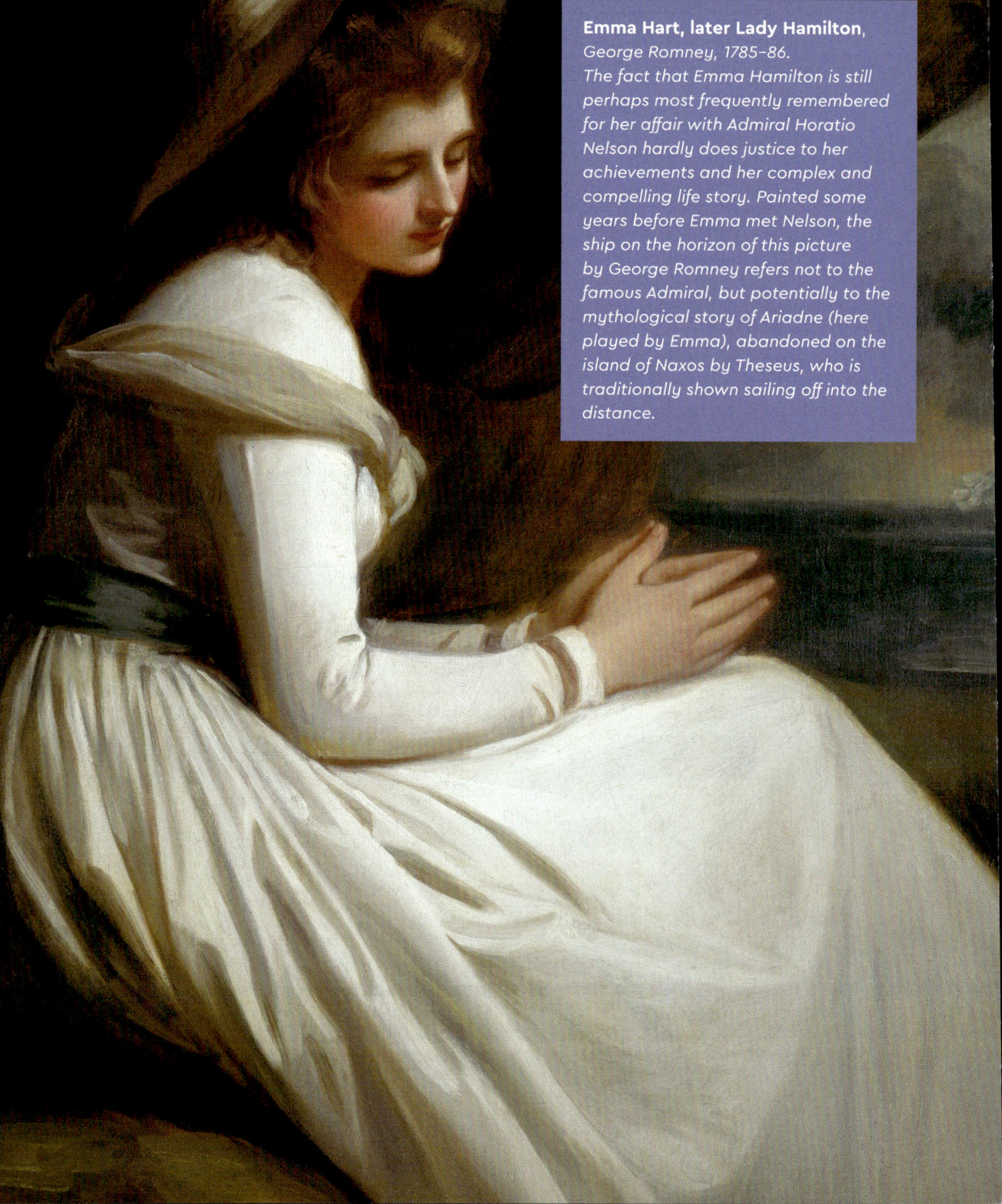

Emma Hart, later Lady Hamilton, *George Romney, 1785–86.*
The fact that Emma Hamilton is still perhaps most frequently remembered for her affair with Admiral Horatio Nelson hardly does justice to her achievements and her complex and compelling life story. Painted some years before Emma met Nelson, the ship on the horizon of this picture by George Romney refers not to the famous Admiral, but potentially to the mythological story of Ariadne (here played by Emma), abandoned on the island of Naxos by Theseus, who is traditionally shown sailing off into the distance.

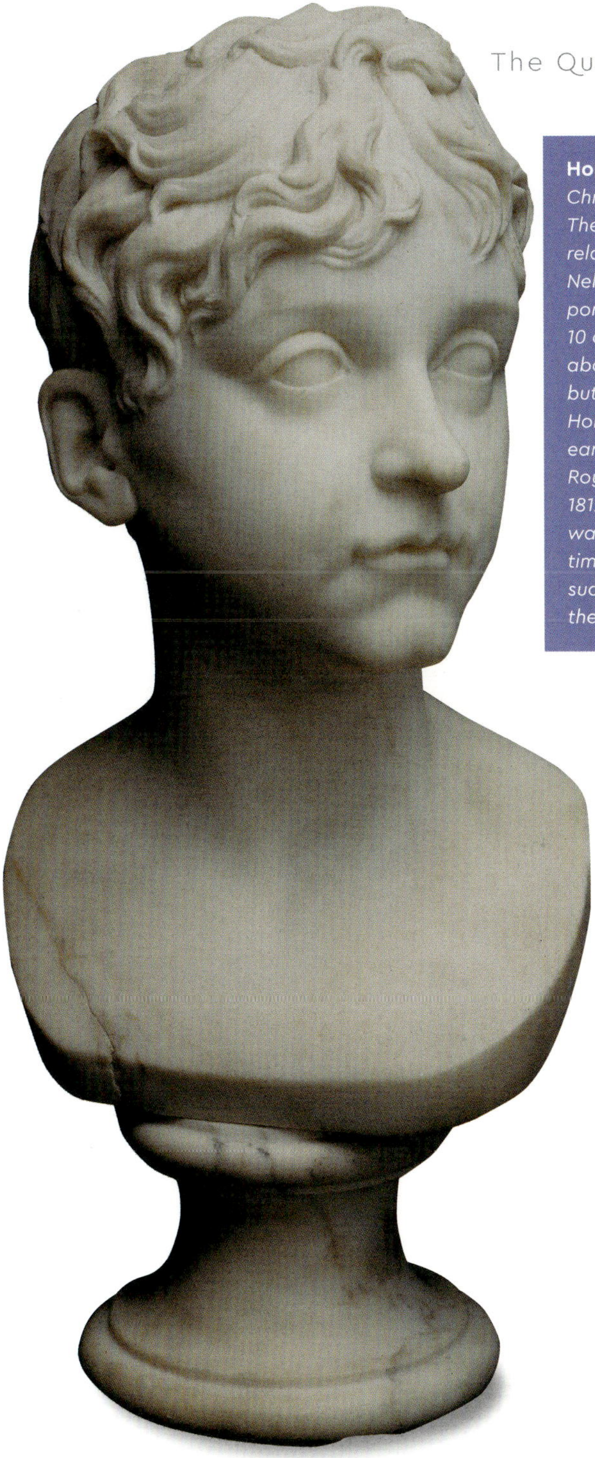

Horatia Nelson, *George Romney, Christopher Prosperi, 1811*
The only child to come of the relationship between Horatio Nelson and Emma Hamilton is portrayed here at the age of 10 or 11. Very little is known about the sculptor Prosperi, but his evident skill at capturing Horatia's youthful features earned the bust a place in the Royal Academy exhibition of 1812. Horatia's cropped hair was highly fashionable at the time and demonstrates that such trends were far from merely the domain of adults.

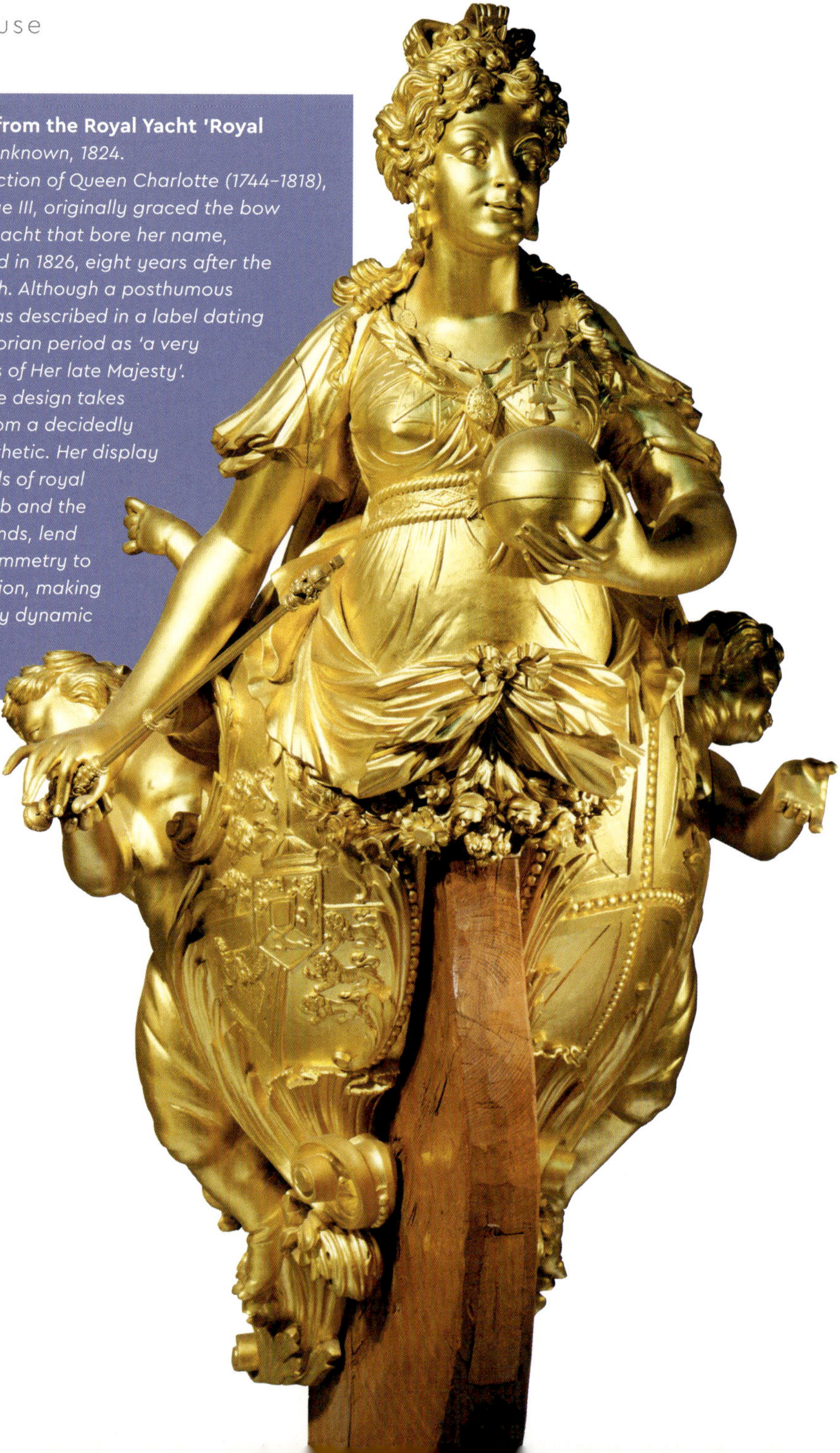

Figurehead from the Royal Yacht 'Royal Charlotte', *unknown, 1824.*
This gilt depiction of Queen Charlotte (1744–1818), wife of George III, originally graced the bow of the royal yacht that bore her name, commissioned in 1826, eight years after the queen's death. Although a posthumous portrait, it was described in a label dating from the Victorian period as 'a very good likeness of Her late Majesty'. The elaborate design takes inspiration from a decidedly baroque aesthetic. Her display of the symbols of royal power, the orb and the sceptre in hands, lend a certain asymmetry to the composition, making it an unusually dynamic figurehead design.

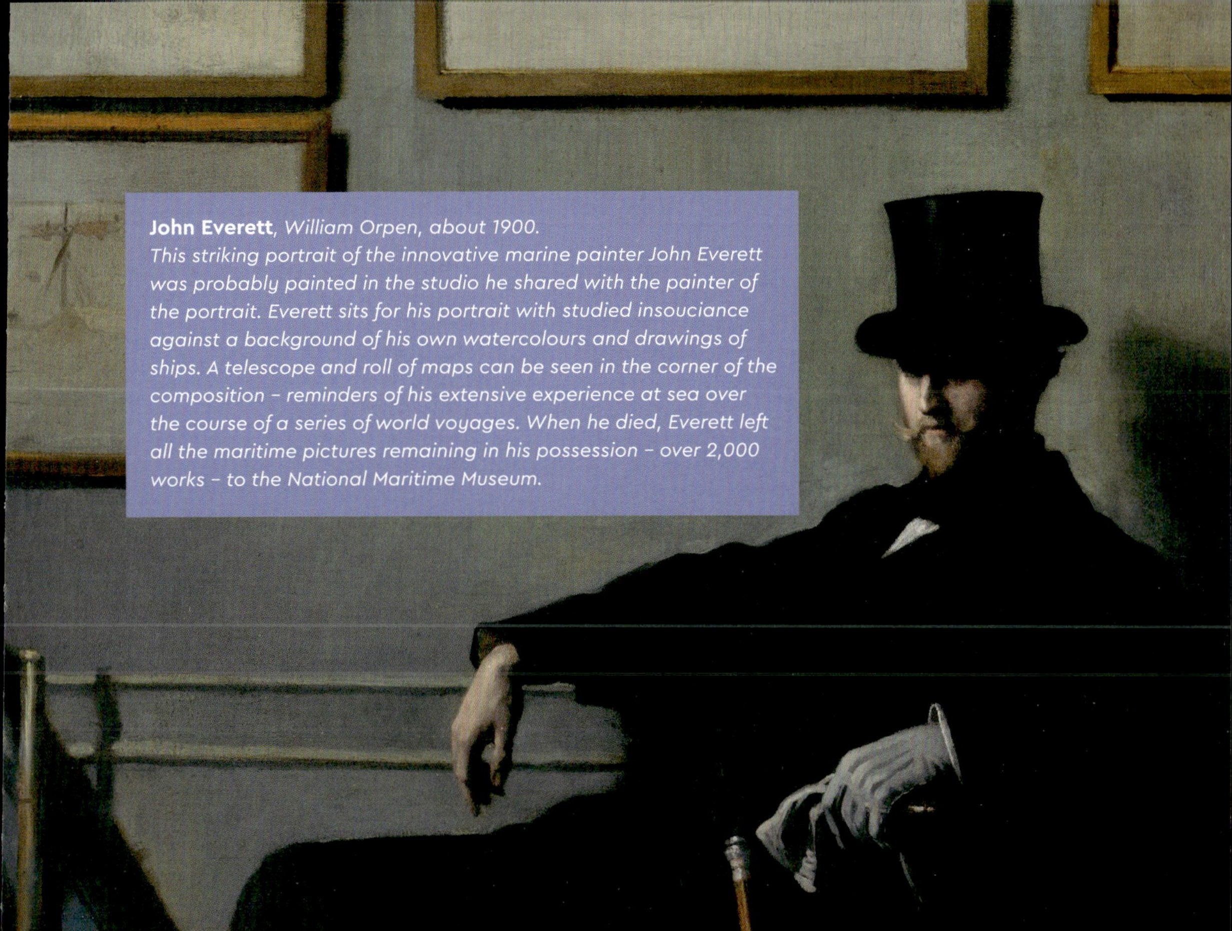

John Everett, *William Orpen, about 1900.*
This striking portrait of the innovative marine painter John Everett was probably painted in the studio he shared with the painter of the portrait. Everett sits for his portrait with studied insouciance against a background of his own watercolours and drawings of ships. A telescope and roll of maps can be seen in the corner of the composition – reminders of his extensive experience at sea over the course of a series of world voyages. When he died, Everett left all the maritime pictures remaining in his possession – over 2,000 works – to the National Maritime Museum.

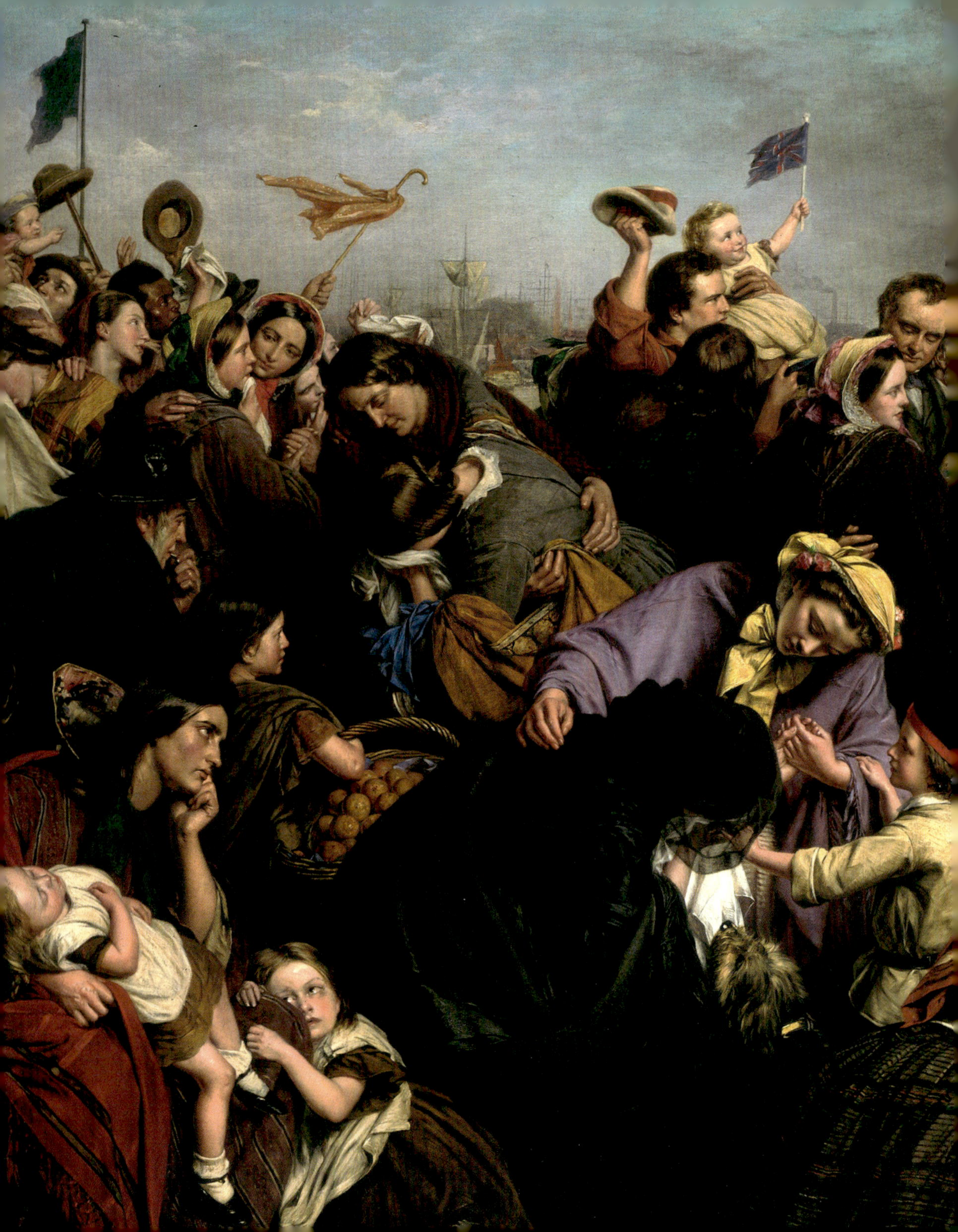

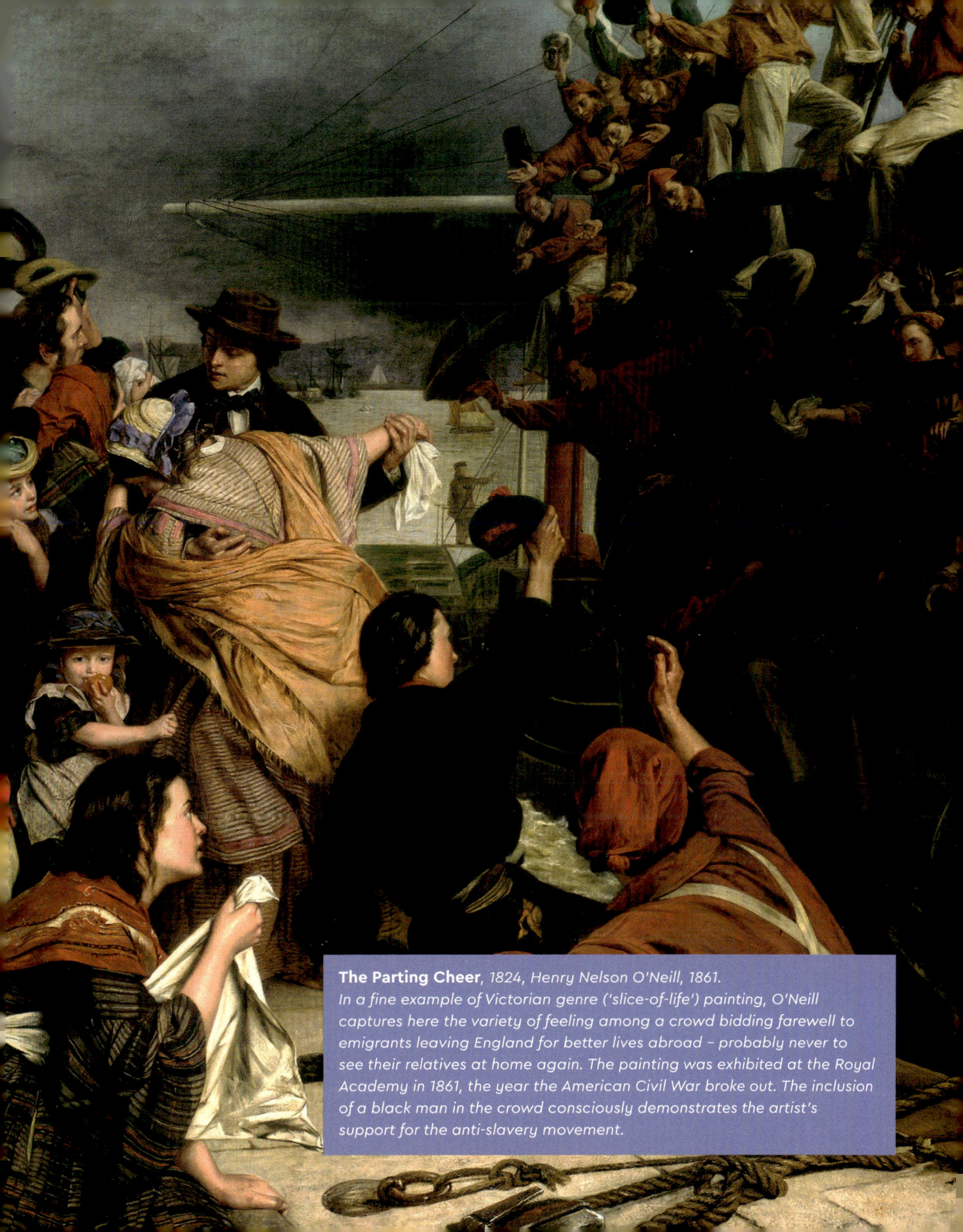

The Parting Cheer, *1824, Henry Nelson O'Neill, 1861.*
In a fine example of Victorian genre ('slice-of-life') painting, O'Neill captures here the variety of feeling among a crowd bidding farewell to emigrants leaving England for better lives abroad – probably never to see their relatives at home again. The painting was exhibited at the Royal Academy in 1861, the year the American Civil War broke out. The inclusion of a black man in the crowd consciously demonstrates the artist's support for the anti-slavery movement.

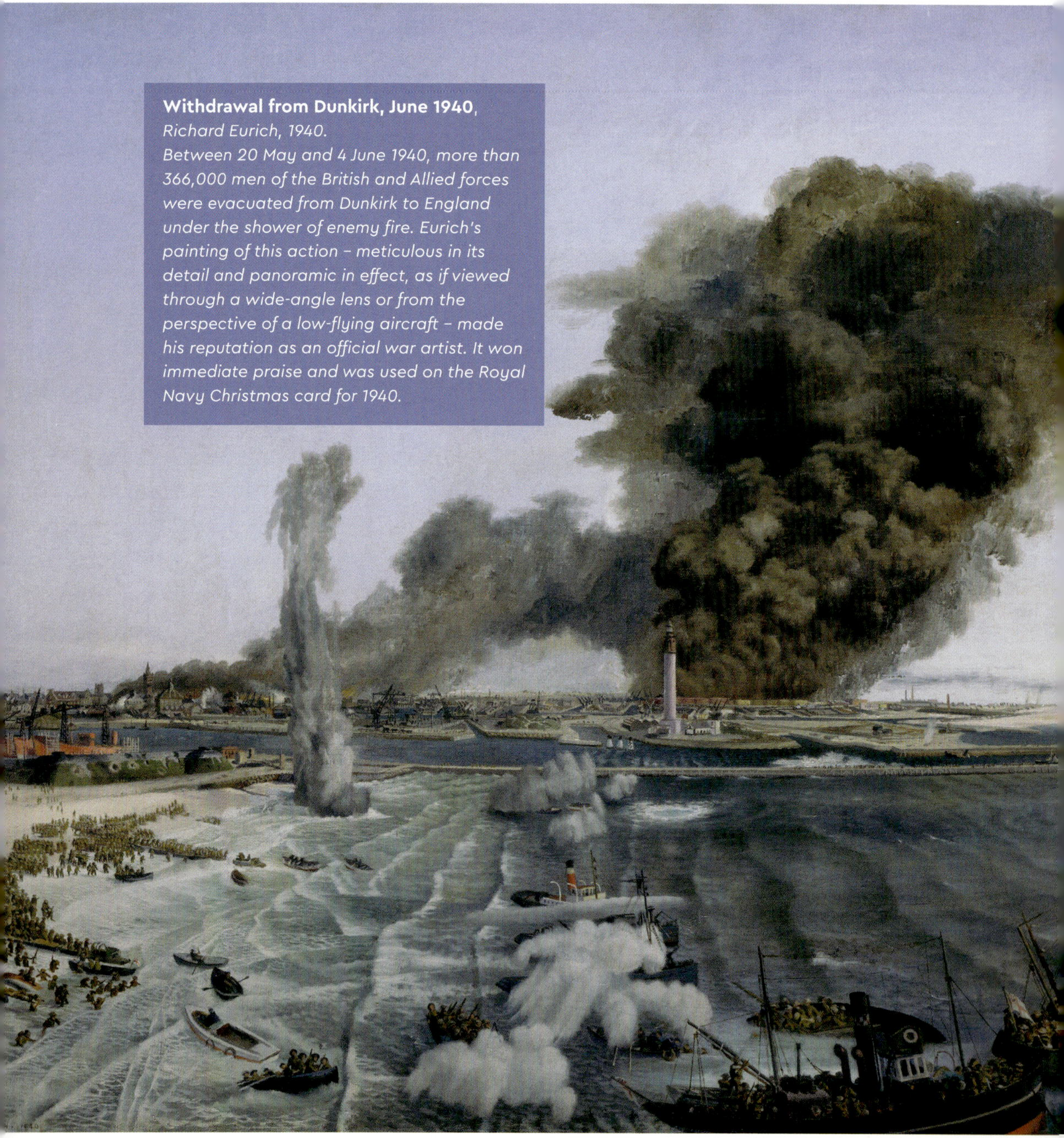

Withdrawal from Dunkirk, June 1940, *Richard Eurich, 1940.*
Between 20 May and 4 June 1940, more than 366,000 men of the British and Allied forces were evacuated from Dunkirk to England under the shower of enemy fire. Eurich's painting of this action – meticulous in its detail and panoramic in effect, as if viewed through a wide-angle lens or from the perspective of a low-flying aircraft – made his reputation as an official war artist. It won immediate praise and was used on the Royal Navy Christmas card for 1940.

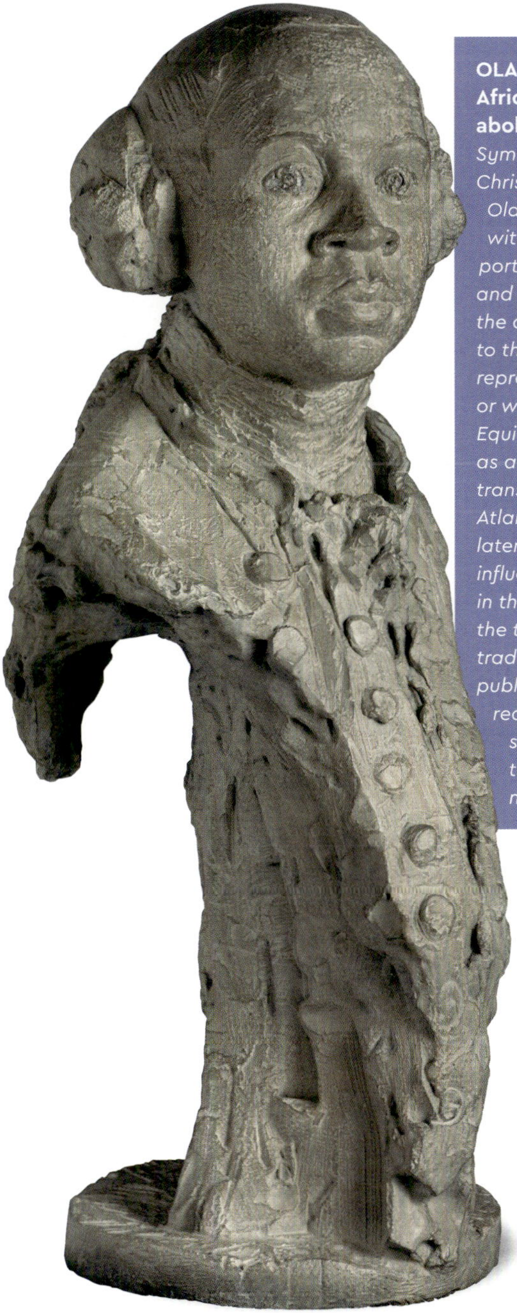

OLAUDAH EQUIANO – African, slave, author, abolitionist, *Christy Symington, 2006.*
Christy Symington's bust of Olaudah Equiano engages with the tradition of portraits of naval figures and seafarers down through the ages, encouraging us to think about who isn't represented in that tradition or who is obscured by it. Equiano, who was enslaved as a child in Africa and transported across the Atlantic to the Americas, later became a highly influential figure in Britain in the campaign to abolish the transatlantic slave trade. His autobiography, published in 1789, provided readers with a new, and shocking, perspective on the realities of Britain's maritime empire.

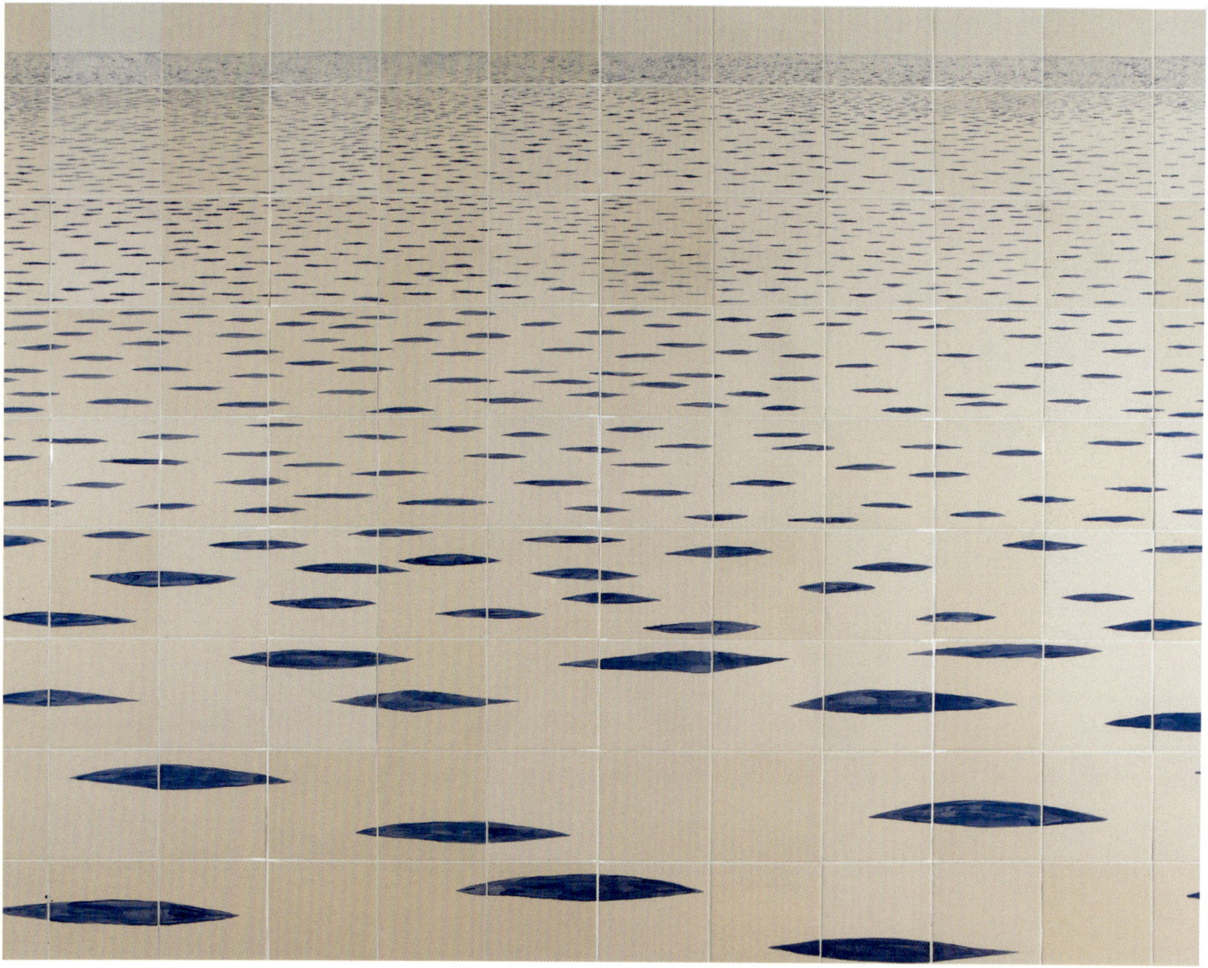

Sea Mark, *Tania Kovats, 2012–14.*
Tania Kovats's Sea Mark draws on the tradition of hand-painted blue and white ceramic tiles, such as this delftware panel. Made up of 113 tiles showing a scene of whaling, the latter would have decorated an early 18th-century Dutch domestic interior, possibly that of a merchant or shipowner. Using a simple, almost abstract form in repetition, Kovats' work is a modern response to the age-old human fascination with the seeming infinity of the ocean.

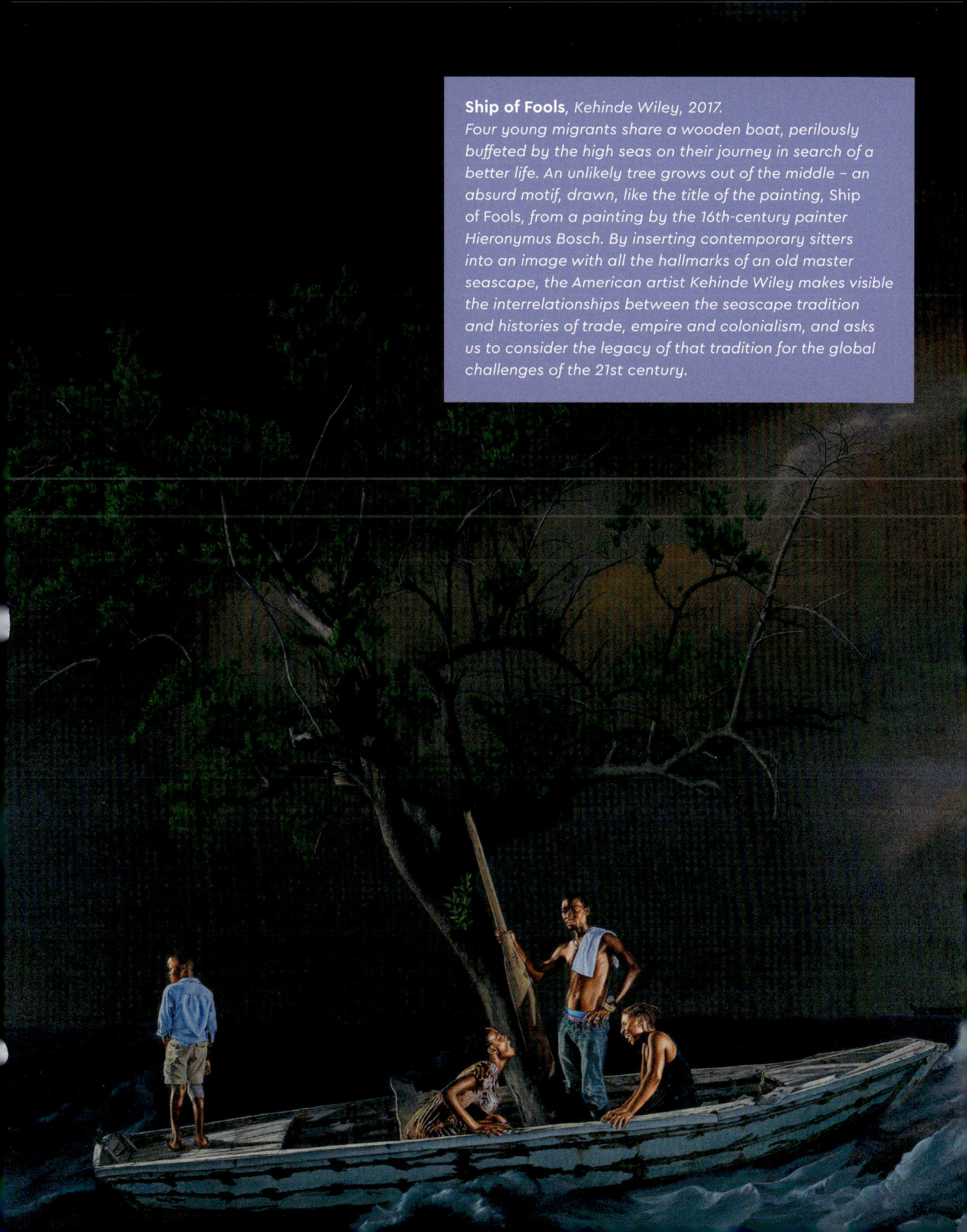

Ship of Fools, *Kehinde Wiley, 2017.*
Four young migrants share a wooden boat, perilously buffeted by the high seas on their journey in search of a better life. An unlikely tree grows out of the middle – an absurd motif, drawn, like the title of the painting, Ship of Fools, *from a painting by the 16th-century painter Hieronymus Bosch. By inserting contemporary sitters into an image with all the hallmarks of an old master seascape, the American artist Kehinde Wiley makes visible the interrelationships between the seascape tradition and histories of trade, empire and colonialism, and asks us to consider the legacy of that tradition for the global challenges of the 21st century.*

Explore more at Royal Museums Greenwich

There's plenty more to see and do at Royal Museums Greenwich. Our museums are all within easy walking distance of each other, and together they offer a culture-filled, fun day out for all ages.

Learning at the Queen's House

Discover a rich variety of talks, activities and performances to complement the permanent and temporary displays in the Queen's House. For more information, go to rmg.co.uk/whats-on.

Support

The valuable support of our Members, Patrons, donors and sponsors allows us to continue our important work through exhibitions, loans, conferences, publications, learning programmes and community initiatives. Please give generously to help us continue this vital work. You can donate at donate.rmg.co.uk. Alternatively, you can donate by credit card by calling the Individual Giving team on +(44) 20 8312 6603, or leave a donation next time you visit. Our donation boxes are located in and around the Museum galleries. Every pound makes a difference.

Membership

If you've enjoyed your day at the Queen's House, Greenwich, why not consider becoming a Member? Enjoy unlimited entry to our four unique attractions: *Cutty Sark*, the Royal Observatory, National Maritime Museum and the Queen's House all year, including free entry to special exhibitions. Membership also includes invitations to private views, special Members' events, discounts in the shop, café and on public events as well as access to a lovely Members' Room and biannual Members' magazine. Members may also purchase an annual guest pass at the Admission desk or from the Membership office. There's really no better way to enjoy the adventure. Visit rmg.co.uk/membership for more information.